A PRIESTLY PEOPLE

A Priestly People

✦✦✦

ROBERT A. BRUNGS, S.J.

SHEED AND WARD : NEW YORK

Contents

Introduction

THE theology of Vatican II has revitalized one of the oldest doctrines of Christianity, that of the priestly people of God. Both in the first letter of St. Peter and in the Book of Revelation the faithful are said to make up a "chosen race, a royal priesthood, a consecrated nation." The very importance that the Fathers of the Council placed on the priesthood of the faithful has proved to be something of an embarrassment. We can intuitively recognize that this concept of the priestly people of God will play a role of critical importance in the renewal of the Church and that an adequate articulation of this doctrine will carry with it the change of many of the structures and forms in the Church as she is presently constituted.

We can glimpse in this priestly designation the stirrings of an authentic yearning for a full sharing on the part of all Christians in the continuing mission of Christ. We know in our hearts that we stand on the brink of a great new life in the Church. We have caught a vision that was present in the early Church—we are all priests and form a nation of men who are consecrated to God. We have heard the thunder of the Spirit but we do not fully understand the message that we have been given. This is our embarrassment.

We are in much the same position as an inventor who does not yet know the value of the discovery that he has made and is still in ignorance of many of the uses to which his invention may be applied. We do not yet realize the riches of the message of the Spirit but we know instinctively that our old concepts are not sufficient to express the message. When we try to fit the rediscovered concept of the priestly people of God into the old fabric of our thought, we find that it just does not fit. True, we can tug here and pull there but we know that it, nevertheless, will not work.

The question keeps coming back. What does it mean to be a priest? The author of the letter to the Hebrews tells us that a priest is essentially a mediator between God and men. His primary task is "to offer gifts and sacrifices" to God in order to reconcile men with God. Through the mediation of the priest, God bestows his gifts and blessings upon men and, through them, their world.

Christ is the high priest without equal. The perfect mediator between God and men, he offered himself to his Father once and for all, and by his mediatorial action effected redemption for all men and for the totality of creation. But what does the Church mean when she calls all Christians priests? Are they really priests or is this merely a way of trying to make the faithful feel a bit more at home in a clerical club? This is a legitimate question and deserves an answer, if any answer can be given at present.

The customary procedure of answering these questions seems to be the attempt to find some points of Christian duty common to both the layman and the cleric. These common elements are then made the links between what, in fact, seem like two priesthoods. This mode of procedure seems directed to the question: how does the priesthood of the faithful relate to the priesthood of the ordained priest? It implies that the prime analogate of the Christian priesthood is the ordained priest. Granted that the ordained priest is a priest, how are the baptized like him?

It seems, however, that this is not the proper question. We should not ask how the priesthood of the faithful fits into the priesthood of orders. This is to put the cart before the horse. The true, operative question is, how can we explain the priesthood of orders in the context of our already priestly lives? We must investigate what the Christian priesthood means and how it arises. Only then will we be able to discuss in any adequate fashion the forms of the priesthood as we know them.

There can be no doubt that the priesthood of the people of God looks to the priesthood of Christ for its meaning and for its mission. Christ's priesthood was not totally a past-oriented reality. It was not exclusively concerned with the reparation of man's fall from familiarity with God. It was, indeed, most deeply committed to the future—to the total remaking of the human race and, with mankind, all of the universe. The mission of Christ's priesthood is as narrow as a single human life and as broad as the cosmos. It looks to the past to repair it and to the future to build the new order of things that the Father revealed in Christ. It was to accomplish these two aspects that Christ lived, died, and rose again from the dead.

In baptism the Christian is incorporated into the life of Christ and, through Christ, into the inner life of the Holy Trinity. He becomes a member of the people of God. He shares Christ's life, Christ's love, and Christ's power. He

shares in the priesthood of Christ and in the mission of
Christ to subdue all of the universe to the will of the Father.
This baptismal sharing in the priesthood of Christ is the
foundation of every mode of priestly work in the Church. All
forms and expressions of the priestly character of the
Church are built firmly on the baptismal priesthood of every
Christian, and each form and expression must be understood
in the context of this priesthood. In other words, the prime
priestly reality in the Church is the priesthood of the faithful, and the ordained priesthood must be considered in the
matrix of this broader and deeper reality.

If the priesthood of the Church is established through the
baptismal sharing of the priesthood of Christ, it is further
specified and made functional by the sacraments of confirmation and orders. The Christian priesthood is established
in baptism, and its activity is specified in confirmation and
orders. These three sacraments are, as it were, the Church-
building sacraments. These sacraments establish the Church
and orient her to the fulfillment of the mission of Christ and
the mission of the Spirit according to the Father's will. In
these three sacraments we see the Church as the created and
finite expression of all of the divine activity.

Baptism gives us a participation in the inner life of the
Triune God; we are really the sons of the Father. Confirmation is the sharing in the Pentecostal outpouring of the Spirit
on the Church. It was the Spirit that drove the disciples from
the upper room into the streets of Jerusalem to preach the
salvation that Jesus had won for all men by his life, death,
and resurrection—the proclamation of the wonderful saving
works of God. The multifaceted mission of the Spirit is the
primary expression of the confirmational priesthood. Orders,

following this synthetic approach, would be the sharing in the temporal mission of the incarnate Son of God. Christ came to redeem, to forgive sin as a preliminary to the building of the kingdom of God. This redeeming still goes on through the priesthood of orders, through those who have been given an official sharing in the Headship of Christ.

In brief, it may be said that the confirmational priesthood shares in the mission of the Spirit and the ordained priesthood participates in the mission of Christ. It is obvious that the mission of the Spirit could not take place without the prior mission of Christ. The mission of Christ, on the other hand, would have remained radically incomplete without that of the Spirit. This really says no more than that the Body of Christ would not be complete if it were all Head or all members. There is a mutual completeness brought about by the confirmational and ordained priesthoods. In them the totality of the divine activity in creation is summed up in a created manner.

In summary, then, the baptismal sharing in Christ establishes the priestly state in the Church, while confirmation and orders direct the priestly activity that is our obligation as members of the priestly people of God. All Christian priests, whatever their specific function, must be united in every phase of the Christian life if the totality of the divine activity is to be represented in some created, though mysterious, way. Only in the mutual presence of the ordained and nonordained is the whole Church present.

The consideration of the Christian priesthood in the conceptual context given above will offer a new orientation both of the baptismal priesthood and of the ordained priesthood. Not all of the ramifications of this conceptualization are apparent. But, in general, it demands the mutual presence of the confirmational and ordained priesthoods in every legitimate aspect of human life. It looks to the cooperation of the members and of those who share in the Headship of Christ in every facet of human activity for the growth and ultimate fulfillment of the kingdom of God. It places the burden of the completion of Christ's mission to restore all of creation to the Father squarely on the shoulders of every Christian priest. It also, finally, agrees with the statement of Paul that in Christ there is no slave or free man, no Jew or Greek, no male or female. In Christ, and in his priestly work, we are all one. We all share in the one mission of Christ, which is to restore all things in love to the Father.

A PRIESTLY PEOPLE

1. The Old Testament Background

HUMAN history is the story of the intervention of God into man's life and growth. From the beginning God has been active, slowly leading man toward his destiny. The Old and New Testaments are the story of God's progressive revelation of himself to man. In this tale of God's concern for man's progress, we see God teaching and guiding man back to himself. The story is one of gradual growth, of rejection, and of repentance on the part of mankind. But in this story we reach the point of a sudden and utterly incomprehensible leap in God's self-revelation. The slow and tortuous interplay between God and creation suddenly, it would seem, culminated in the earthly appearance of God-made-man.

God became incarnate and, as St. John tells us, dwelt among us. We Christians are certain that the incarnation was a momentous event in the history of God's activity among men. We have no doubt that this has changed the history of man and has even changed the manner of divine intervention in history. But do we really very often stop to think of just how momentous an event this was? Do we ever stop to ask ourselves just what change this event introduced? Do we wonder why Christ took on a human nature and became like us in all things except sin?

The scope of one's vision of Christianity depends almost totally on his understanding of the incarnation. Why, indeed, did Christ come on earth? Was it merely to repair the damage caused by man's primal sin and to remove all the degradation that flowed from this fall from familiarity with God? Or was there a further and deeper purpose? Could it be that Christ would have become man even if man had not rejected God's love-overtures? Revelation is silent on this question, at least to the extent that it does not directly treat it. The scripture is more concerned in telling us what God has done and rarely enters into a discussion of why God did it.

This question concerning the purpose of the incarnation is extremely important for an understanding of Christianity and for the fullest development of a vision of Christian life and Christian purpose. Our purpose in life as Christians should bear some relationship to Christ's purpose in becoming and remaining man. For this reason it would seem helpful to look quickly at the course of salvation history to see if we can get some indications of an answer to the question of the purpose of Christ's incarnation.

There can be absolutely no doubt that Christ came to repair man's sin. Scripture is clear beyond dispute about this. Man had fallen from his state of familiarity with God, and because of this he was radically cut off from God's love. Man had said "no" to God's love, and until God said "yes," the dialogue was closed. Man could not by his own volition reopen it. He could not engage God's attention until God himself made the approach. Man is limited to responding to the divine initiative, either positively or negatively. He is never the initiator of any relationship with divinity.

Man's negative response to God, his refusal to recognize his own limitation and his duty to serve, trapped him within the fragile shell of his own being. He became a prisoner within the walls of his own person, within the bleak and sterile confines of selfishness. Once the familiar love with God had been lost, there was no way to regain it. To use the biblical imagery of Genesis, it was God who walked with Adam and Eve in the Garden amid the cool breezes of evening. It was not Adam and Eve who walked with God.

The familiar contact between creature and Creator was the result of an overture on God's part. It was in no way initiated at the desire of the creature. After the fall of man, we are told, man was expelled from the garden; he was cut off from intimate contact with God. It is not so much that Adam and Eve were driven from the Garden; rather, it could be better stated that God left the Garden, and without his loving presence it became a sterile, barren, and hostile place in which to live.

Indeed, without God's company and supportive love Eden became a place of thistles and thorns, a land of pain and toil, a desert where once it had been fertile, a recalcitrant land that had to be broken to the will of man rather than a cooperative land which yielded to man, as it were, of its own accord. Man, divorced from familiarity with God, confined by his own inbuilt limitation, and bound down by his own petty vision of reality, could not see anything beyond himself and beyond those things which he had chosen to call his own. Man became a prisoner locked within himself and was to be the more pitied because he was his own jailer.

St. Paul describes the consequences of this fall from love and from the domination of nature.

The Law, of course, as we all know, is spiritual; but I am unspiritual; I have been sold as a slave to sin. I cannot understand my own behaviour. I fail to carry out the things I want to do, and I find myself doing the very things I hate. . . . In fact, this seems to be the rule, that every single time I want to do good it is something evil that comes to hand. In my inmost self I dearly love God's law, but I can see that my body follows a different law that battles against the law which my reason dictates. That is what makes me a prisoner of that law of sin which lives inside my body (Rom. 7:14-15; 21-23).

But even with sin man was not left totally destitute. Though he had fallen from friendship with God, man still had a potential for growth. He had not lost his precious gift of self-awareness and the power for growth which springs from it. Through his self-awareness and intellectual power he could still slowly come to dominate nature. Over the period of many millennia he came to exercise greater control over his environment. He built a few rude huts and gathered with other men into small communities. He learned some crude methods of agriculture, and in time he was able to settle down and to cease the continuous nomadic life of the hunter. He no longer had to follow the migration of animals to survive. Within these small communities man learned to share with others the labor that survival demanded. With a common sharing of labor there came a modicum of leisure to pursue occupations other than those directly concerned with the mere continuance of life.

Man, relieved from the laborious struggle for survival, found deep within himself the genius to create. Now that there was some time to think and to question, man's curiosity about his surroundings began to mature and to play a larger part in the community's life and outlook. The innate sense of beauty that is man's began to express itself in decorations, even in the embellishment of tools, of weapons, and of other necessities such as pottery. He became concerned not only with how well a thing worked but also with how beautiful it was. Man's poetic gift expressed itself in language of rare beauty. His curiosity pressed him forward on a search for the meaning of life. As he became aware of the vastness of the universe, he began to question his place in it. He looked for answers to the ultimate questions: who and what and why am I? His poetry and artistry and other forms of expression were attempts on his part to locate himself in the vast sweep of the cosmos.

While some men concerned themselves with questions of cosmic importance and while others concerned themselves with the creation of articles of, at first, a primitive beauty, still others learned to build with a surer skill. Dwellings became more permanent, larger, and more beautiful. The activities of these men and their growing artistry, coupled with their desire for possession and permanence, led to buildings of enormous proportions and of stunning beauty. Even thousands of years after their construction the pyramids have not lost their power to overwhelm men with their gigantic size, and even the ruins of other works show a beauty that has not as yet been surpassed. Men looked beyond the earth to the heavens and discovered a few of its secrets, thus beginning the search into the mystery of mat-

ter. Courageous men began to explore the wonders of the
earth and set out from their homes in search of adventure,
wealth, power, and knowledge.

Other groups of men busily engaged themselves in the
development of weapons and were able to hunt for food
with greater effectiveness and relatively greater safety. Some
learned the methods of extracting various metals from ore
and the techniques of working these new materials. Man,
however, saw that these materials were suited to destroy as
well as to build. He became a more efficient killer, and war
took on an uglier and more brutal aspect. He subjected his
neighbors if he could, or else was subjected by them.

In an almost ceaseless campaign across the then civilized
world the Assyrians conquered Egypt, only to be conquered
by the Babylonians. Other nations grew in power and top-
pled those who had earlier risen to dominate large areas of
land. The Persians, Medes, Greeks, and Romans—each in
turn—subjected vast areas of the world and imposed their
wills on the subject lands. Man became more tyrannical, and
words such as *genocide* found a place in his vocabulary.

In the course of man's history all was not completely bad
or completely good. Man continued to progress, and in some
aspects of human endeavor he produced works of surpassing
beauty and of permanence. Still, as Paul says,

. . . they knew God and yet refused to honour him as God or to
thank him; instead, they made nonsense out of logic and their
empty minds were darkened. The more they called themselves
philosophers, the more stupid they grew, until *they exchanged
the glory* of the immortal God for a worthless imitation, *for the
image* of mortal man, of birds, of quadrupeds and reptiles. . . . In

other words, since they refused to see it was rational to acknowl-
edge God, God has left them to their own irrational ideas and to
their monstrous behaviour. And so they are steeped in all sorts of
depravity, rottenness, greed and malice, and addicted to envy,
murder, wrangling, treachery and spite. Libellers, slanderers,
enemies of God, rude, arrogant and boastful, enterprising in sin,
rebellious to parents, without brains, honour, love or pity. They
know what God's verdict is: that those who behave like this
deserve to die—and yet they do it; and what is worse, encourage
others to do the same (Rom. 1:21-23; 28-32).

So, man progressed and grew, but not completely. He
slowly matured and began the process of conquering the
universe—but for himself and not in relation to the purpose
of the universe's Creator. He used his gifts to create beauty
and to search into nature and into himself, but the essential
relation to God was lacking, at least in great part. Man, cut
off from God, had lost the power that the vision of God and
of God's creative purpose would have given him. Man's
familiarity with God, a relationship offered to man by God
himself, had been rejected and annulled by man. His horizon
now bounded by himself, his desires, and his purposes, he
had lost the cosmic view of himself as lord-steward over
creation. He had attempted to set himself up as absolute
ruler over the universe and had ended up subject to the
tyranny of his own limitation.

But God, even though he was rejected by man, did not
totally abandon him. Though his love-overture had fallen on
the deaf ears and hard heart of man and even though his
offer of love had been judged inferior to created things, God
would not allow the rejection of his love to be the last word
in his dialogue with man. God still walked with him, but

now in a different way. Just as God had spoken the first word in the dialogue between himself and man, so he could not allow man to speak the last word.

Man's "no" met with a "yes" from God. He refused to accept the rejection as definitive.

Through the centuries God continued to walk with man and slowly and patiently revealed himself to man. As a teacher, God led man closer to himself, a little at a time. As a lover, God showed a delicacy which is the touchstone of true love. He drew man closer to himself in a way calculated not to overwhelm man or to deprive him of the freedom that is God's highest gift. God spoke to man and showed him his presence in a way that man could understand. Little by little his voice became clearer, his message a bit more compelling, and his presence somewhat more apparent.

One day God spoke to a man from Haran, a town to the northwest of Mesopotamia, and said to him, "Leave your country, your family and your father's house, for the land I will show you. I will make you a great nation; I will bless you and make your name so famous that it will be used as a blessing. I will bless those who bless you: I will curse those who slight you. All the tribes of the earth shall bless themselves by you" (Gen. 12:1-3). Abram, hearing God's word and acting on it, left his home, and with his wife, his nephew, and his servants, he set out for the land of Canaan. His life over the period of the next several years was nomadic. He left Canaan and traveled into Egypt during a time of famine in Canaan. Finally, he returned from Egypt and settled in the land that God pointed out to him. Here he prospered greatly. But Abram's wife was barren, and he had no heirs except those children born to his slave-girls.

When Abram was ninety-nine years old Yahweh appeared to him and said, "I am El Shaddai. Bear yourself blameless in my presence, and I will make a Covenant between myself and you, and increase your numbers greatly." Abram bowed to the ground and God said this to him, "Here now is my covenant with you; you shall become the father of a multitude of nations. You shall no longer be called Abram; your name shall be Abraham, for I make you father of a multitude of nations. I will make you most fruitful. I will make you into nations, and your issue shall be kings. I will establish my Covenant between myself and you, and your descendants after you, generation after generation, a Covenant in perpetuity, to be your God and the God of your descendants after you" (Gen. 17:1-7).

God in this intervention revolutionized his way of acting toward man. He committed himself in a solemn way to act in Abraham's behalf. He even changed Abram's name to Abraham. Among ancient peoples a name did more than indicate a person. It made a thing what it was, and the changing of a man's name meant the change of his destiny. The new name meant a new future. From this time on God would honor the alliance that he had made with Abraham.

Abraham would have, God told him, a son by his wife Sarah who was barren and beyond the age of childbearing. God fulfilled the promise he had made, and a son was born to Abraham and Sarah. The son, Isaac, was the seal on the covenant between God and man. God had pledged himself to be Abraham's protector, to walk with him and act in his interests, to bless him and his descendants. Through his relationship with Abraham, solemnly confirmed on both sides by the covenant, God offered to man the restoration of the familiarity that had characterized his relations with man before the primal sin. With Abraham's affirmative response to him, God again walked with man in familiar love.

Abraham's descendants multiplied and prospered. In a time of famine they went to Egypt and were able through the influence of Joseph to secure high positions at the court of Pharaoh. In time, however, the dynasty of Pharaoh was overthrown, and the new Pharaoh "knew not Joseph." Abraham's posterity became slaves under a regime that grew more oppressive as time passed. But God, always faithful to his convenant, in time raised up a man to deliver this group of people from the tyranny of their Egyptian overlords. He called Moses and sent him back into Egypt, from which he had fled, to tell Pharaoh to free the Hebrews.

And Yahweh said, "I have seen the miserable state of my people in Egypt. I have heard their appeal to be free of their slave-drivers. Yes, I am well aware of their sufferings. I mean to deliver them out of the hands of the Egyptians and bring them up out of that land to a land rich and broad, a land where milk and honey flow. . . ." Moses said to God, "Who am I to go to Pharaoh and bring the sons of Israel out of Egypt?" "I shall be with you," was the answer "and this is the sign by which you shall know that it is I who have sent you . . . After you have led the people out of Egypt, you are to offer worship to God on this mountain. . . . Go and gather the elders of Israel together and tell them, 'Yahweh, the God of your fathers, has appeared to me—the God of Abraham, of Isaac, and of Jacob; and he has said to me: I have visited you and seen all that the Egyptians are doing to you. And so I have resolved to bring you up out of Egypt where you are oppressed, into the land of the Canaanites, the Hittites, the Amorites, the Perizzites, the Hivites and the Jebusites, to a land where milk and honey flow'" (Ex. 3:7-8; 11-12; 16-17).

Moses, with a great deal of fear and trepidation, returned from Sinai to his homeland in Egypt. After much strife and conflict the Israelites were finally allowed by the Egyptian authorities to leave the land where they were oppressed. Moses led them through the desert to the neighborhood of Mount Sinai.

Moses then went up to God and Yahweh called to him from the mountain, saying, "Say this to the House of Jacob, declare this to the sons of Israel, 'You yourselves have seen what I did with the Egyptians, how I carried you on eagle's wings and brought you to myself. From this you know that now, if you obey my voice and hold fast to my covenant, you of all the nations shall be my very own for all the earth is mine. I will count you a kingdom of priests, a consecrated nation.' Those are the words you are to speak to the sons of Israel." So Moses went and summoned the elders of the people, putting before them all that Yahweh had bidden them. Then all the people answered as one, "All that Yahweh has said, we will do." And Moses took the people's reply back to Yahweh (Ex. 19:3-8).

At Sinai, God and Israel entered into a solemn covenant. The people promised to obey the commandments which God had just given them, and God, in his turn, promised to be with them, to give them the land flowing with milk and honey, to be their guardian and protector, to be their savior. So long as Israel observed God's statutes, so long as they were true to the covenant of Sinai, God fulfilled his promise to protect them and give them land and prosperity.

But even before Israel left the desert and reached the borders of the Promised Land, they, his own people, turned their back on him. By worshiping the golden bull at Sinai and by grumbling against God who was leading them, they turned away from the covenant which God had ratified with them at Mount Sinai. This was to be the history of the covenant-relationship between God and Israel—faithlessness followed by repentance which was again followed by more faithlessness. Despite their backsliding, despite their hardness of heart, God still dwelt among them in the Tent of Meeting, their place of worship. God had promised to be with them, and God always honors his pledge.

So long as Israel observed God's commandments and kept its covenant-promises, it prospered and grew stronger. The Israelites conducted a slow but successful compaign to conquer Canaan from its inhabitants. After they had consolidated their hold on the land they had won, they were able to turn their attention to those works which brought them prosperity and wealth. With prosperity came a turning away from God and a forgetting that it was the Lord who had led them and helped them. The people of God turned to the worship of the Canaanite fertility gods and goddesses.

In return God withdrew his protecting hand from them, and their neighbors were successful in winning back territory from Israel. With adversity there came to the Israelites a remembrance of the promises that Yahweh had made to them, and they turned once more to God, asking forgiveness and seeking help. In these times of national crisis Yahweh raised up Judges, men like Gideon and Samson, to lead Israel to victory over its enemies. Despite Israel's continual turning from him in times of peace and prosperity and despite its continual lapsing into idolatry, God always responded favorably when his people turned to him and asked his help.

In time, God welded Israel into a single nation under a king. At first the experiment was successful, and Israel grew to the peak of its power and prestige under David and Solomon. But once again the story was the same. With power and wealth the nation turned to reliance on treaties with Egypt or Assyria or whoever seemed to be the dominant power of the moment. They put their faith not in the power and faithfulness of Yahweh but in the horses of Egypt or the chariots of Assyria.

God sent prophets to direct the kings and the people, but the prophets were killed for saying things that those in authority did not want to hear. And the sorry tale of man's infidelity to God went on through the destruction of Jerusalem, the exile in Babylon, and even the return to Palestine after the Babylonians were defeated. Kings misled the people, the prophets were unsuccessful, and the priests and pharisees who led the people of God after their return from exile were poor guides.

The history of Israel and of the working out of the covenant-relation of Sinai is a vivid commentary on God's fidelity to his promises and on man's infidelity to the promises he had made with God. In time of tribulation the Israelites always turned to God, but in time of peace and prosperity the people of God ran after foreign alliances and worshiped foreign gods. The Old Testament, the history of the relationship of God with his people, is a sad commentary on man's lack of fidelity to God and to his will.

The question arises, however, as to what would have resulted had Israel perfectly observed the covenant which it had accepted at the foot of Mount Sinai. While it is true that an answer to such a question cannot be more than hypothetical, it is still profitable to investigate the question since its consideration is valuable for an appreciation of the meaning of the incarnation.

After the covenant was ratified, God dwelt in the midst of his people. In the desert, before Israel ended its nomadic way of life and settled in the Promised Land, God dwelt in some mysterious way in the Tent of Meeting.

The cloud covered the Tent of Meeting and the glory of Yahweh filled the tabernacle. . . . At every stage of their journey, whenever the cloud rose from the tabernacle the sons of Israel would resume their march. If the cloud did not rise, they waited and would not march until it did. For the cloud of Yahweh rested on the tabernacle by day, and a fire shone within the cloud by night, for all the House of Israel to see. And so it was for every stage of their journey (Ex. 40:34; 36-38).

When the people of Israel settled down after the conquest of the Promised Land and came under the rule of their own kings, a magnificent temple was built on the holy mountain, on Mount Zion.

Then Solomon called the elders of Israel together in Jerusalem to bring the ark of the covenant of Yahweh up from the Citadel of David, which is Zion. . . . Now when the priests came out of the sanctuary, the cloud filled the Temple of Yahweh, and because of the cloud the priests could no longer perform their duties: the glory of Yahweh filled Yahweh's Temple. Then Solomon said: "Yahweh has chosen to dwell in the thick cloud. Yes, I have built you a dwelling, a place for you to live for ever" (1 Kings 8:1; 10-13).

After the dedication of the Temple the Lord appeared to Solomon.

When Solomon had finished building the Temple of Yahweh and the royal palace and all he had a mind to build, Yahweh appeared to Solomon a second time, as he had appeared to him at Gibeon. Yahweh said to him, "I grant your prayer and the entreaty you have made before me. I consecrate this house you have built: I place my name there for ever; my eyes and my heart shall be always there. For your part, if you walk before me with innocence of heart and in honesty, like David your father, if you do all I order you and keep my laws and my ordinances, I will make your royal throne secure over Israel for ever, as I promised David your father when I said: You shall never lack for a man on the throne of Israel" (1 Kings 9:1-5).

God, therefore, dwelt in the midst of the Israelites, and it would seem that if Israel had followed the commands and ordinances of the Lord, he would have dwelt forever in their midst. Is it inconceivable to think that, if Israel had faithfully observed the covenant, the familiarity with God, lost by man's primal sin, might have been restored to the Israelites through the favor of God? God lived in the Temple in a relationship of some familiarity, and his presence among the people was symbolized by the Holy of Holies. God was with them but was still relatively unapproachable.

He lived with them, if we may use the analogy, in a neighborly relation, much as the king of Israel lived among the common people. The king did not associate with the people but remained aloof from the masses. God's relation to the Israelites was of this nature. Only once a year was the high priest permitted to enter into the Holy of Holies. The Hebrews called God "Father," but this was not expressed in the familial vocabulary later used in the New Testament. God was their father, as the king was their father, the one they trusted to look after their interests and to provide them with prosperity and the opportunity to live a life secure from their enemies. It does not seem entirely unreasonable to suppose that if Israel had honored the covenant and had fully observed the statutes of the Lord, this relationship would have become deeper and more familiar.

Indeed, this seems to be the message of the prophets.

That is why I am going to lure her and lead her out into the wilderness and speak to her heart. I am going to give her back her vineyards, and make the Valley of Achor a gateway of hope. There she will respond to me as she did when she was young, as she did when she came out of the land of Egypt. When that day comes—it is Yahweh who speaks—she will call me, "My husband", no longer will she call me, "My Baal" [i.e., master]. . . . I will betroth you to myself for ever, betroth you with integrity and justice, with tenderness and love; I will betroth you to myself with faithfulness, and you will come to know Yahweh (Hos. 2:14-16; 19-20).

If we take these words at face value, words echoed by prophet after prophet, we must assume that God would have entered into a union of deep intimacy with man. It does not seem too fanciful to presume that God, within the context of the Old Testament revelation, might have restored man to his primal intimacy with God. The Old Testament could have reached fulfillment in the relationship of familiarity with God that man once possessed.

In the relationship between God and man as recorded in

the pages of the Old Testament one can see a rising crescendo in God's activity on behalf of man. After man had fallen from God's favor and cut himself off from God's love, there was a period when God seemed to have worked solely on an individual basis with men. Then, God made a covenant with Abraham that established a community of salvation. This covenant was observed by God and was most vividly manifested in the exodus of the Israelites from bondage in Egypt. The covenant was formalized at Mount Sinai, and the people of God ratified it. It is conceivable that the reparation of the breach between God and man could have been accomplished by the perfect observance of the Mosaic Law. The Law could have fulfilled God's purpose completely, had God's purpose been merely the reparation of the bond of intimacy that man had originally been given by God.

But God did not view the old covenant as the end of his saving activity among men. He sent his Son, enfleshed and "like unto a son of man," into the world and in so doing abrogated the old covenant and replaced it with the new covenant ratified by the blood of his Son. The old covenant was the establishment of a relationship of familiarity between God and men. The new covenant looked to something further—to the raising up of sons of God and to the establishment of a familial relationship between God and men.

2. The Incarnation

NOW as they were eating, Jesus took some bread, and when he had said the blessing he broke it and gave it to the disciples. "Take and eat;" he said "this is my body." Then he took a cup, and when he had returned thanks he gave it to them. "Drink all of you from this," he said "for this is my blood, the blood of the covenant, which is to be poured out for many for the forgiveness of sins" (Mt. 26:26-28).

THE REMEDY OF THE PAST

In the book of the Acts, we read, " 'You must repent,' Peter answered 'and everyone of you must be baptised in the name of Jesus Christ for the forgiveness of your sins, and you will receive the gift of the Holy Spirit' " (Acts 2:38). We read also in Paul that Christ came, lived, and died to free men from their bondage to sin and death.

God's justice that was made known through the Law and the Prophets has now been revealed outside the Law, since it is the same justice of God that comes through faith to everyone, Jew and pagan alike, who believes in Jesus Christ. Both Jew and pagan sinned and forfeited God's glory, and both are justified through the free gift of his grace by being redeemed in Christ Jesus who was appointed by God to sacrifice his life so as to win reconciliation through faith. In this way God makes his justice known; first, for the past, when sins went unpunished because he held his hand, then, for the present age, by showing positively that he is just, and that he justifies everyone who believes in Jesus (Rom. 3:21-26).

Such quotations could be multiplied almost without end, but there is little need to do so. It is clear to all that Christ came to offer himself for the sins of men, to assume the burden of their weakness and of their guilt, and to accept in their behalf the punishment of the Father. The Acts of the Apostles (Chapter 8) applies to Christ the prophecy of Isaiah about the Suffering Servant.

And yet ours were the sufferings he bore, ours the sorrows he carried. But we, we thought of him as someone punished, struck by God and brought low. Yet he was pierced through for our faults, crushed for our sins. On him lies a punishment that brings us peace, and through his wounds we are healed. We had all gone astray like sheep, each taking his own way, and Yahweh burdened him with the sins of all of us (Is. 53:4-6).

The enfleshed Son of God came to bring man back to God, to restore to him the familiar relationship that had been lost through his sinfulness. In the person of Christ, God walked again with man in as complete and intimate a way as possible. Christ destroyed the bondage in which sin held man and restored him to God's love. Man could now approach God as he had once been able to walk and talk with God amid the cool breezes of the evening in Eden. Man was again free to look beyond himself and to see something beyond the horizon of his own goals and desires. He could again glimpse a reality for himself beyond his own limitations and could aspire to things he could not have even dreamed of before.

But God's second gift of life to man far surpassed the first gift. St. Paul dwells on this at length.

Adam prefigured the One to come, but the gift itself [the reconciliation through Christ] considerably outweighed the fall. If it is certain that through one man's fall so many died, it is even more certain that divine grace, coming through the one man, Jesus Christ, came to so many as an abundant free gift. The results of the gift also outweigh the results of one man's sin: for after one single fall came judgement with a verdict of condemnation, now after many falls comes grace with its verdict of acquittal (Rom. 5:15-16).

Paul indicates in this passage that Christ gave back to man more than he had lost through Adam's sin. God had created man with a self-awareness and a potential above that of other creatures. He had also given man a gift to which he could not of himself aspire—familiarity with God. God, if we may speak in these terms, made himself a neighbor to man. Had man not sinned, this intimacy could have been expected to deepen and to broaden. Man and God could have grown into a stronger and more binding love-union. But it was not God's design in the incarnation merely to restore what was lost. In the enfleshing of the Son of God, the Father revealed his desire to raise up a race of sons, not neighbors. The relation of familiarity was, in Christ, superseded by a familial relationship. Christ did not come merely to restore what had been lost. The gift that God gave man in the enfleshing of his Son was above and beyond anything that man had ever possessed.

MEANING FOR THE PRESENT

The incarnation was not intended to be nothing more than a "patch-job" on creation. God, as has been said, desired more than a return to something he had already given man. The Father wished more than just the forgiveness of sins. It is perfectly true that this forgiveness was the necessary base on which the new order of things was to be established. The building that God wished to construct could not rise on uncleared ground. But clearing the ground is only the first step —important, yes, but not everything. The temple, built from "living stones," in which God was to dwell far surpassed anything previously conceived by man or previously revealed by God.

The revelation of the Son and the giving birth to other sons was the secret that had lain hidden in God from all eternity, finally to be revealed in Christ. With the coming of Christ, man entered into a new era, a new order of things, one in which he was to enter into a familial relationship with God. The use in the New Testament of the word *Abba* is indicative of the change that occurred with the incarnation. An Old Testament Jew would not have called God by this familiar and affectionate title. About as close as we can come in English to this title would be "Dad." This is the kind of union which God has, in Christ, established with men. We may address the Father with the intimacy of a member of the family. We are sons, truly sons, and we should not hesitate to think of the Father in terms of affection and of love.

This familial union between men and God is exactly what Christ came to establish.

We know from scripture that God had ordained from all eternity that a race of sons be raised up to be heirs to his kingdom.

You have been taught that when we were baptised in Christ Jesus we were baptised in his death; in other words, when we were baptised we went into the tomb with him and joined him in death, so that as Christ was raised from the dead by the Father's glory, we too might live a new life. If in union with Christ we have imitated his death, we shall also imitate him in his resurrection (Rom. 6:3-5).

Everyone moved by the Spirit is a son of God. The spirit you received is not the spirit of slaves bringing fear into your lives again; it is the spirit of sons, and it makes us cry out "Abba, Father!" The Spirit himself and our spirit bear united witness that we are children of God. And if we are children we are heirs as well: heirs of God and coheirs with Christ, sharing his sufferings so as to share his glory (Rom. 8:14-17).

Here, and in several other places, Paul gives us a view of the positive purpose which motivated the incarnation. A full view of the scriptural message presents us with a tremendously exciting prospect. God created the universe as an expression of his own fullness and infinite richness and beauty. In a finite expression of himself and of his love, he cast into the primal void countless images of his own infinite self-giving, each of these images reflecting in some created way the love and beauty of the Creator.

The primal gas congealed into stars and galaxies, and in at

least one of those galaxies one of the stars developed a planetary system of its own. On at least one of the planets of that galaxy conditions were finally suitable for the emergence of life. Life appeared, and through the eons which followed, the forms of life became more complex and much more highly structured. Through this growing complexity the earth witnessed the development of the various kinds of plant life and finally the myriad forms of sentient life. The stage was finally set for the emergence of human life, for the appearance of a creature who showed self-awareness and an intelligence that raised him above all other animals.

God entered into a relation of friendship with this creature. Man, as a conscious being and one aware of himself, was capable of conscious self-giving to another. He was capable of love. He could deliberately and freely give of himself, his resources, and his time for the welfare of another. In the context of the divine initiative men could enter into a relationship of friendship and love with God. With his unique integration of the material and the spiritual, man was made the hinge-being in creation. If all creation was directed back to the hand of God from which it issued, if through some minimal or rudimentary form of self-giving creation itself imitated divine self-giving, then man was the necessary link between material creation and God. Man, as the integration of matter and spirit, could, by conscious self-giving, help to lead all of creation back to God.

But mankind, of its own power and potential, could not bridge the gap between creation and Creator. Even if man had fully responded to the divine love-initiative, the question could still be raised as to whether creation could be fully reunited to the Creator. In the union of spirit and matter in man, God had formed a link between two worlds. But in this union of spirit and matter, creation and the Creator were not yet united in the intimacy desired by God. It is important for our purposes to consider this question only in the context of the data we have from scripture.

We know from the New Testament that God desired a race of sons, heirs to his kingdom and coheirs with Christ to the richness of the divine life. It was to this end that Christ became man. God's plan for creation could be fulfilled not by the union of spirit and matter in man but only by the union of human nature and divinity in Christ. We can see here the growing divine intervention in the universe which God had created and preserved. From matter creation moved to life and from the crude early forms of life to a form that was apt for union with the spiritual. But even this was not enough to satisfy the divine desire. God's purpose was fulfilled only with the imposition of divinity on human nature. This was the incarnation.

In man God united the worlds of spirit and matter. In Christ we have the union of creation and Creator. God the Father, as is evident from the New Testament, desired the complete and unalterable union of creation with himself. In the God-man we have the union of spirit-matter infinitely deepened and broadened by union with divinity. In Christ we have the bridge between creation and God. This, more than the forgiveness of sins, was the purpose of the incarnation. Forgiveness was the necessary preliminary to God's purpose, but it remained only something preliminary. The new order of things, built to be sure on the deliverance of men from the rule of sin, looks far beyond the mere reparation for man's primal fall.

ORIENTED TO THE FUTURE

It is clear from scripture that Christ rose from the dead and ascended bodily into heaven. These events did more than put the seal of God's approval on Christ's redemptive death. Rather, these events are the definitive acceptance of creation into the very life of the Trinity. Christ, with his death and resurrection, did not give up his humanity. If the life, death, and resurrection of Christ had been directed solely to the reparation of man's sins, what reason would there have been for the ascension of Christ into heaven? Why would he have kept his body once its purpose was served? If the incarnation looked chiefly to the past, the ascension would seem to have been a superfluous action on the part of God. But the ascension is actually God's acceptance of matter into his being.

God, in Christ, has now and always will have a body. In Christ the union of creation and Creator reached its greatest possible intimacy. In the one person, Christ, God united divine nature with human nature and, through this human nature, with all of creation. It is as the God-man that Christ rules in heaven.

I [John] turned round to see who had spoken to me, and when I turned I saw seven golden lamp-stands and, surrounded by them, a figure *like a Son of man,* dressed in a long robe tied at the waist with a *golden girdle. His head and his hair* were *white as white wool* or as snow, *his eyes* like a *burning* flame, *his feet like burnished bronze* when it has been refined in a furnace, and *his voice like the sound of the ocean.* In his right hand he was holding seven stars, out of his mouth came a sharp sword, double-edged, and his face was like the sun shining with all its force.

When I saw him, I fell in a dead faint at his feet, but he touched me with his right hand and said, "Do not be afraid; it is I, *the First* and *the Last;* I am the Living One, I was dead and now I am to live for ever and ever, and I hold the keys of death and of the underworld" (Rev. 1:12-18).

It is not difficult from passages such as this to see that it is as a man that Christ will judge and rule. Paul tells us much the same thing.

Because that is what he [the Father] has done: he has taken us out of the power of darkness and created a place for us in the kingdom of the Son that he loves, and in him, we gain our freedom, the forgiveness of our sins. He is the image of the unseen God and the first-born of all creation, for in him were created all things in heaven and on earth: everything visible and everything invisible, Thrones, Dominations, Sovereignties, Powers—all things were created through him and for him. Before anything was created, he existed, and he holds all things in unity. Now the Church is his body, he is its head. As he is the Beginning, he was first to be born from the dead, so that he should be first in every way; because God wanted all perfection to be found in him and all things to be reconciled through him and for him, everything in heaven and everything on earth, when he made peace by his death on the cross (Col. 1:13-20).

Here and elsewhere in Paul we catch a glimpse of the cosmic sweep of the incarnation. Christ came both to forgive sins and to reconcile to God all things on earth and in heaven. Christ reigns in heaven and is actively engaged in the continuing endeavor to subject all things to the Father. In joining divinity to matter in Christ, the Father revealed his will to unite all of creation to himself.

In the incarnation, God joined himself to creation. In the resurrection and ascension into heaven, God definitively ratified this union. Humanity was accepted as part of the God-life, and with humanity matter was irrevocably joined to the divinity. God had definitively accepted a body and had unalterably decreed the sacredness of all creation. If man is indeed the summation of all the eons of evolution and if Christ remains man in heaven, then God in raising Christ into glory has shown his will that all creation be united to him in his glory. It cannot be overstressed that Christ's enfleshment and his mission did not end with the Good Friday events. This would have sufficed were the forgiveness of sin the primary concern of the Father. But, in fact, this was not the end nor has the end come yet.

Christ's mission will not be completed until everything is subject to and united to the Father.

Just as all men die in Adam, so all men will be brought to life in Christ; but all of them in their proper order: Christ as the first-fruits and then, after the coming of Christ, those who belong to him. After that will come the end, when he hands over the kingdom to God the Father, having done away with every sovereignty, authority and power. . . . And when everything is subjected to him, then the Son himself will be subject in his turn to the One who subjected all things to him, so that God may be all in all (1 Cor. 15:22-24; 28).

We—at least some of us in the western Church—may perhaps have come to consider that the incarnation looked first and foremost to the past sorry story of man's dialogue with God. In fact, it seems clear from scripture that Christ's enfleshment was primarily concerned with the future glorious story of man's growing love affair with God. The Christ-mystery looks more to man's growing sense of responsibility as a son who is to inherit the kingdom of his Father. It looks to the growing maturity of man, the Church, and the universe.

We, perhaps, have come to consider Christ's incarnational activity to have come to an abrupt halt with his ascension into heaven. Do we not, more often than not, look on Christ as passively sitting on a throne at the right hand of the Father? We would never admit that he does not care what happens to us and to the Church, but do we ever consider him as still actively engaged in the continuing struggle for dominion over the universe? Do we imagine him as even more active in the world of men and in directing man's history than he was when he was seen and heard and felt on earth? Yet we know from Paul that Christ is still striving to attain his full stature.

In one sense Christ's victory has been secured, and Christ has come to his full maturity. In another sense this growth to maturity continues. This is merely an expression of a basic tension or polarity that has always existed in Christianity. As early in Christian theology as St. Paul's Epistles this polarity showed itself. Paul himself speaks of Christ having achieved our deliverance and having attained victory over sin and death.

But he also speaks, especially in his last epistles, Ephesians and Colossians, of the growing Christ struggling to attain maturity and working to subject all things to the Father, to bring all of creation back to the Father.

And to some, his gift was that they should be apostles; to some, prophets; to some, evangelists; to some, pastors and teachers; so that the saints together make a unity in the work of service, building up the body of Christ. In this way we are all to come to unity in our faith and in our knowledge of the Son of God, until we become the perfect Man, fully mature with the fullness of Christ himself (Eph. 4:11-13).

We cannot divorce the incarnation from the mission of the Holy Spirit who is the vivifying element in the growth of Christ's Body. The Church, enlivened and directed by the very Spirit of God, is the prolongation of Christ and of Christ's mission in time and space. The Church is the continuation of Christ's mission to subject all things to the Father and to bring all created things to union with the Father in and through Christ. This mission of the Spirit, meaningless apart from the birth, death, resurrection, and ascension of Christ, will continue until the day when Christ returns to take the subjected universe from our hands and in turn places it in the hands of the Father.

But we must see the work of the Church in terms of the work of Christ, in terms of the future progress of humanity, as well as in terms of the forgiving of man's sins. The Spirit testifies to our spirits that we are sons and, as sons, heirs to the kingdom of God. The Spirit directs us to see the values of growth and development and helps us to recognize those things which lead rather to man's decline and weakening. The Spirit gives us the strength to serve mankind in love and shows us how this love is to be expressed.

This is all done in the context of the Church, the prolongation of Christ and his mission. The love needed for the growth of mankind, the love that is the earthly manifestation of the Spirit, cannot be separated from the Church. The Church is really the extension of the incarnation, the Body of

Christ that is struggling toward maturity, that is straining to grow into the integration of what is human in her with what is divine. Christ, through the Church, is more active in the affairs of men than he ever was when he walked among the men of Palestine two thousand years ago.

FOUNDATION OF OUR HAPPINESS

There is still another aspect of the incarnation to be considered. Scripture tells us often that God dwells in inaccessible light.

Moses said, "Show me your glory, I beg you." And he [God] said, "I will let all my splendour pass in front of you, and I will pronounce before you the name Yahweh. I have compassion on whom I will, and I show pity to whom I please. You cannot see my face," he said "for man cannot see me and live." And Yahweh said, "Here is a place beside me. You must stand on the rock, and when my glory passes by, I will put you in a cleft of the rock and shield you with my hand while I pass by. Then I will take my hand away and you shall see the back of me; but my face is not to be seen" (Ex. 33:18-23).

It should be clear from this citation and from many like it in both the New and Old Testaments that God the Father is totally beyond the grasp of man.

Also, it would seem strange if once we attained heaven, we would be able to dispense with our complete dependence on Christ. This would seem to relegate our relation to Christ to the category of sheer use. It would be almost as if we could discard Christ as we would discard an old pair of shoes after we had worn them for a long and wearying journey. It is more fitting that our relationship of total dependence on Christ would continue into eternity. After all, Christ is the way, the truth, and the life. There is absolutely no reason to believe that he will cease to be such for us in glory.

It is true that it is in Christ that we are made sons. It is in and through Christ that we become members of the Trinitarian "family life." In Christ, but only in Christ, do we become "sharers in the divine nature" (2 Pet. 1:4). Our dependence on Christ for our "divineness" shall never end. There can never come a time when we shall be able to live a life of shared divinity independent of Christ. Our beatitude can never be separated from our life in Christ.

In terms of our beatitude it can be asked whether it is accidental that Christ retained his body after he ascended into heaven. Does it not seem fitting that Christ's bodily ascension into heaven would play an important role in our knowledge of the Father? In heaven we will be able to know and love Christ in his humanity. We will be able to see Christ and hear him and touch him. We will remain men in heaven—our salvation is not a process of "angelization." If this were the case, one could legitimately ask why God enfleshed himself instead of "defleshing" us. In fact, if one were to hold to some sort of angelization process, he would have great difficulty reconciling his thought with the dogma of the resurrection of the body.

If a person were to read the speech of Paul on the Areopagus, he would be struck with the reactions of the Athenians to Paul's mention of Christ's resurrection.

"Since we are the children of God, we have no excuse for thinking that the deity looks like anything in gold, silver or stone that has been carved and designed by a man. God overlooked that sort of thing when men were ignorant, but now he is telling everyone everywhere that they must repent, because he has fixed a day when the whole world will be judged, and judged in righteousness, and he has appointed a man to be the judge. And God has publicly proved this by raising this man from the dead." At this mention of rising from the dead, some of them burst out laughing; others said, "We would like to hear you talk about this again." After that Paul left them, but there were some who attached themselves to him and became believers, among them Dionysius the Areopagite and a woman called Damaris, and others besides (Act 17:29-34).

Over the centuries we have, without explicitly denying the dogma of our bodily resurrection, made heaven a rather "antiseptic" place, uncontaminated by the germs of materiality. We talk of "direct vision of God" as if it were only a purely intellectual process, unsullied by emotion or bodily reaction. Perhaps Christ's resurrection and ascension were meant to keep us from falling too deeply into this Neoplatonic pit. We shall have a direct vision of God, but will it be one that is purely and totally intellectual? God forbid! This would, it seems, effectively deny Christ's sanctification of all of creation and would make a dead letter of God's unalterable and definitive acceptance of matter into the Godhead. No, it seems we must accept the fact that we are, and always will be, men.

We will see and hear and touch Christ. We will be in an intimate love-union with Christ through his humanity. In knowing and loving Christ as man (and in the mutual expression of that love), we know and love Christ as God, since in Christ humanity and divinity exist in a completely and totally integrated unity. In knowing Christ as man we know him as God. When we know Christ as God, we know the Father, since Christ is the perfect image of the Father. It is as if the blinding light of the Father were refracted for us through the perfect prism that is Christ. We then, as it seems we should, come to know and love the Father through Christ, who is God-with-us.

In summary, then, it can be said that the incarnation is a supratemporal reality, completely overcoming all limits of time. It is really the "new wine" which the old wineskin of time could not contain. The incarnation looks to the past, to removing the debilitating effects of sin from man. It has reopened man's path to God by removing the obstacles that man had erected but could not then remove. It fully repaired man's offense against God and reestablished the covenant between God and men. It undid man's rebellion against God and rebuilt the relationship of familiarity.

The incarnation also looks to the present, to our being made sons of God. It looks to our being made sharers of the divine life and of the divine love. It is the "new state of things" which has replaced the state of man's sinfulness and has far surpassed man's state of original innocence. It is the time in which Christ calls us his "brothers and sisters." It looks to a present situation which Paul describes:

Having this hope [of a life of greater glory], we can be quite confident; not like Moses, who put a veil over his face so that the Israelites would not notice the ending of what had to fade. And anyway, their minds had been dulled; indeed, to this very day, that same veil is still there when the old covenant is being read, a veil never lifted, since Christ alone can remove it. . . . It will not be removed until they turn to the Lord. Now this Lord is the Spirit, and where the Spirit of the Lord is, there is freedom. And we, with our unveiled faces reflecting like mirrors the brightness of the Lord, all grow brighter and brighter as we are turned into the image that we reflect; this is the work of the Lord who is Spirit (2 Cor. 3:12-18).

It is because of the incarnation that Paul can say,

Now that that time has come we are no longer under that guardian [the Law], and you are, all of you, sons of God through faith in Christ Jesus. All baptised in Christ, you have all clothed yourselves in Christ, and there are no more distinctions between Jew and Greek, slave and free, male and female, but all of you are one in Christ Jesus. Merely by belonging to Christ you are the posterity of Abraham, the heirs he was promised (Gal. 3:25-29).

In virtue of the incarnation our task is one of growing into Christ, of integrating our humanity and the divinity which we have come to share in baptism. Our task is one of revealing Christ to each other and to the world.

I [Paul], who am less than the least of all the saints, have been entrusted with this special grace, not only of proclaiming to the pagans the infinite treasure of Christ but also of explaining how the mystery is to be dispensed. Through all the ages, this has been kept hidden in God, the creator of everything. Why? So that the Sovereignties and Powers should learn only now, through the Church, how comprehensive God's wisdom really is, exactly according to the plan which he had had from all eternity in Christ Jesus our Lord. This is why we are bold enough to approach God in complete confidence, through our faith in him; so, I beg you, never lose confidence just because of the trials that I go through on your account: they are your glory. This, then, is what I pray, kneeling before the Father, from whom every family, whether spiritual or natural, takes its name: Out of his infinite glory, may he give you the power through his Spirit for your hidden self to grow strong, so that Christ may live in your hearts through faith, and then, planted in love and built on love, you will with all the saints have strength to grasp the breadth and the length, the height and the depth; until, knowing the love of Christ, which is beyond all knowledge, you are filled with the utter fulness of God (Eph. 3:8-19).

The incarnation, then, continues in the present in the Church, which is the prolongation of Christ in space and time. It continues also in all who with faith in Christ have been baptized into his death and who have risen with him and who now live in him. In us, united to Christ and living a life of shared divinity, the incarnation continues through the work of the Spirit of Christ and of the Father. Christ in us, through the Spirit who gives us life and directs us, continues the work of "making all things new."

In our present work, so long as that work is built on Christ's work, the incarnation looks also to the future of mankind. In Christ we are engaged in building the new temple on the cornerstone which is Christ.

By the grace God gave me [Paul], I succeeded as an architect and laid the foundations, on which someone else is doing the building. Everyone doing the building must work carefully. For the foundation, nobody can lay any other than the one which has already been laid, that is Jesus Christ. On this foundation you can build in gold, silver and jewels, or in wood, grass and straw, but whatever the material, the work of each builder is going to be clearly revealed when the day comes. That day will begin with fire, and the fire will test the quality of each man's work. If his structure stands up to it, he will get his wages. . . . (1 Cor. 3:10-14).

If we are engaged in building and strengthening the kingdom that Christ founded while he was on earth, and if the completed kingdom of Christ is heaven, then in a quite real way the temple we are now building is heaven.

The incarnation also looks to the ordering of all creation to the Father's will. All this has not yet been accomplished and the enfleshment of Christ, which is a still continuing reality, looks toward this final goal of the subjection in love of all things to the Father.

I think that what we suffer in this life can never be compared to the glory as yet unrevealed, which is waiting for us. The whole creation is eagerly waiting for God to reveal his sons. It was not for any fault on the part of creation that it was made unable to attain its purpose, it was made so by God; but creation still retains the hope of being freed, like us, from its slavery to decadence, to enjoy the same freedom and glory as the children of God. From the beginning till now the entire creation, as we know, has been groaning in one great act of giving birth; and not only creation, but all of us who possess the first-fruits of the Spirit, we too groan inwardly as we wait for our bodies to be set free. For we must be content to hope that we shall be saved—our salvation is not in sight, we should not have to be hoping for it if it were—but, as I say, we must hope to be saved since we are not saved yet—it is something we must wait for with patience (Rom. 8:18-25).

The incarnation, as we see from Paul, is directed to the liberation from decay of the children of God and of all the universe with them.

Finally, the incarnation plays a vital role in our blessedness in heaven when we shall see and hear and, in some mysterious way, touch God. We shall be able to embrace Christ, and he will be able to hold us close to himself. The incarnation looks forward to that definitive stage of man's history which St. John has described in such beautiful poetry.

Then I saw *a new heaven and a new earth;* the first heaven and the first earth had disappeared now, and there was no longer any sea. I saw the holy city, and the new Jerusalem, coming down from God out of heaven, as beautiful as a bride all dressed for her husband. Then I heard a loud voice call from the throne, "You see this city? Here God lives among men. He will make *his home among them; they shall be his people,* and he will be their God; his name is *God-with-them. He will wipe away all tears from their eyes;* there will be no more death, and no more mourning or sadness. The world of the past has gone." Then the One sitting on the throne spoke: "Now I am making the whole of creation new" he said. "Write this: that what I am saying is sure and will come true." And then he said, "It is already done. I am the Alpha and the Omega, the Beginning and the End. I will give water from the well of life free to anybody who is thirsty; it is the rightful inheritance of the one who proves victorious; and *I will be his God* and *he a son to me*" (Rev. 21:1-7).

3. The Priesthood of Christ

AS it was his purpose to bring a great many of his sons into glory, it was appropriate that God, for whom everything exists and through whom everything exists, should make perfect, through suffering, the leader who would take them to their salvation. For the one who sanctifies, and the ones who are sanctified, are of the same stock; that is why he openly calls them *brothers* in the text: *I shall announce your name to my brothers, praise you in full assembly.* . . . Since all the *children* share the same blood and flesh, he too shared equally in it, so that by his death he could take away all the power of the devil, who had power over death, and set free all those who had been held in slavery all their lives by the fear of death. For it was not the angels he took to himself; he took to himself *descent from Abraham.* It was essential that he should in this way become completely like his brothers so that he could be a compassionate and trustworthy high priest of God's religion, able to atone for human sins. That is, because he himself has been through temptation he is able to help others who are tempted (Heb. 2:10-12; 14-18).

It is clear from this passage that the incarnation and Christ's priesthood are intimately related. This is made even clearer in the same Epistle.

No one takes this honour [high priesthood] on himself, but each one is called by God as Aaron was. Nor did Christ give himself the glory of becoming high priest, but he had it from the one who said to him: *You are my son, today I have become your father,* and in another text: *You are a priest of the order of Melchizedek, and for ever.* During his life on earth, he offered up prayer and entreaty, aloud and in silent tears, to the one who had the power to save him out of death, but he submitted so humbly that his prayer was heard. Although he was Son, he learnt to obey through suffering; but having been made perfect, he became for all who obey him the source of eternal salvation and was acclaimed by God with the title of high priest *of the order of Melchizedek* (Heb. 5:4-10).

It was as man that Christ assumed his priesthood. It was his humanity, as the Epistle to the Hebrews tells us, that qualified him for the office of high priest. This humanity was his from the first moment of his conception. This does not at all mean to imply that Christ's priesthood necessarily reached its full term and full effectiveness at the moment when he was conceived. We are forced by scripture itself to admit that Christ grew as man. "And Jesus increased in wisdom, in stature, and in favour with God and men" (Lk. 2:52). Before considering Christ's priesthood it may perhaps be of value to consider the implications of the possibility of growth in Christ.

First, it would seem to be unfaithful to the scriptural evidence to deny the possibility of growth in Christ. The

Epistle to the Hebrews tells us that "It was essential that he should in this way become completely like his brothers" (Heb. 2:17). For men, growth is a law of life and even, perhaps, our greatest gift from God. There is no reason why Christ should have been exempt from this creaturely condition. Had he been so exempt, would not his humanity have been merely a sham? Had Christ possessed full physical, intellectual, and emotional maturity from the moment of conception, what meaning would his life have for us?

We are all willing to admit physical growth in Christ because scripture has given us a few references to his birth and youth. But does not scripture also tell us that he grew in wisdom? What kind of man would he have been, had he not been subject to the limitations to which every other man must be subject? To view Christ as serenely in possession of every human perfection to its fullest degree would seem to make Christ a human anomaly. Yet scripture tells us in no uncertain terms that he was not an anomaly—he was like us. Does not a view of Christ as above growth deny the reality of his incarnation? Could he really be said to have been made man if he had been a psychological law totally unto himself? Is not Christ human because he took on a humanity just like ours?

We cannot deny that the union of God and man in Christ was complete on the ontological level from the moment of his conception. There was never a moment when the incarnate Christ was not fully God and fully man. The union between divinity and humanity was perfect from the beginning. It would not seem appropriate for Christ to have been able to become more God or more man as time went by. This does not necessarily mean, though, that there was no opportunity for his human awareness of this union to grow. It does not necessarily imply that Christ was not able to grow in psychological awareness of his true dignity and true personality. It seems from scripture that this is the exact process of growth that Christ underwent. Some scripture scholars tell us that Christ's human awareness of his messianic dignity came to the fore only with his baptism by John on the banks of the Jordan and especially with the revelation of God that immediately followed on this baptism.

It is instructive, also, to note that the times when Jesus is specifically mentioned to have prayed were related to crises in his life. He prayed all night before he chose the disciples (Lk. 6:12-16); he spent the night alone in prayer before he made the decision to leave the vicinity of Capernaum to teach throughout Galilee, "for that is why I came" (Mk. 1: 35-38). On the day of the multiplication of the loaves and fishes, when the people wanted to carry him off to make him king, he went into the hills by himself (Jn. 6:15). At the moment of the supreme crisis of his life, when in the Garden he "began to show grief and distress of mind" (Mt. 26:37), he went apart and prayed for strength to face the coming trial. Is it to be considered accidental that scripture shows Christ praying before and during each of the great moments in his life? Could it have been that he really needed guidance and help and strength from his Father? These are questions to be pondered deeply.

If Christ indeed grew and lived out in his life the process of integration of his humanity and divinity, then we must expect that Christ grew in the awareness of his priestly office. This, again, is not to imply that there was ever a moment when he was not the priest of the new covenant nor is it to imply that there was an act of his that was not a priestly act. Christ was, in theological terms, substantially a priest. The priesthood was his in virtue of his very being. At every moment and in every way he is priest. This is his nature. Because of this, Christ is priest in a way that is radically different from every other priest.

Christ by his very life is a priest; all other priests are given the office at some time or other for a period of time in order to perform certain tasks. For all priests other than Christ the priesthood is an accidental phenomenon. Were a man not to agree to assume the priestly office offered to him, he would still be himself. If Jesus of Nazareth had not agreed to be the priest of the new covenant, he would not be the Christ. To be Christ, in other words, is to be priest.

In his infancy and in his youth Christ was the priest of the new covenant. At his work bench in Nazareth, Christ was fulfilling the priestly office given him by the Father. But as he matured through the growing psychological integration of his divinity and humanity, he became more conscious of his priestly office and what his mission in the world was. So, on the level of his human consciousness Christ's priesthood grew and developed. This growth is reflected in his life, in his leaving the narrow confines of a small Palestinian village at the beginning of his ministry in Galilee, this ministry that was to have an ever broadening scope in Judea and in the lands neighboring on Palestine. It was reflected in his realization that he was the messiah who had been so long promised to Israel and that as messiah he must live out the role of the Suffering Servant described by Isaiah with such touching detail.

This realization was dramatically spelled out in the events

of the Last Supper when Christ perpetuated his priesthood
on earth in the persons of his apostles and their successors.
This priesthood led him to the bloody sacrifice of Calvary—
to crucifixion and death. Yet death was merely a phase in
Christ's priestly work of restoration of all things to the Father. It was not the culminating act of that priesthood, and it
was no more important an act of that priesthood than the
resurrection-ascension action.

Now if Christ raised from the dead is what has been preached,
how can some of you be saying that there is no resurrection of the
dead? If there is no resurrection of the dead, Christ himself cannot have been raised, and if Christ has not been raised then our
preaching is useless and your believing it is useless; indeed, we
are shown up as witnesses who have committed perjury before
God, because we swore in evidence before God that he had
raised Christ to life. For if the dead are not raised, Christ has not
been raised, and if Christ has not been raised, you are still in
your sins. And what is more serious, all who have died in Christ
have perished. If our hope in Christ has been for this life only, we
are the most unfortunate of all people (1 Cor. 15:12-19).

Paul in the above passage leaves no doubt of the importance of the resurrection in the history of man's salvation.
Christ's death, by itself, would not, in the plan of the Father,
have accomplished the forgiveness of man's sins, nor would
it have been sufficient for God's revelation of his decisive
acceptance of creation into the life of the Trinity. We must
be careful never to concentrate all our attention on any one
event or even any single phase of Christ's life. In much of
our thinking we have come to regard the crucifixion as the
high point of Christ's life and have seemingly considered the

resurrection-ascension mystery a sort of an appendage. This may be a reflection of the comparative silence of the four Gospels about the risen life of Christ.

Still, as Paul tells us, if Christ was not raised from the dead, our faith is vain and empty. The life of Christ and, consequently, his priesthood cannot be focused exclusively on his death. We must broaden our view to include with his death the resurrection and the ascension. We should not even limit our view to these three major events. All the events of Christ's life play a part in our understanding of his priesthood. Nazareth has a role in Christ's priesthood, although that role may not be so important as his death, resurrection, and ascension. We cannot really understand the full import of his priesthood if we ignore any of its aspects.

It has been pointed out that Christ is priest by the very fact of his existence. What was the moving force behind this priesthood? What was it that made his mediation acceptable to the Father? Was it the death on the cross? Partly, yes. But this is not the full answer. Paul, in Philippians, says,

In your minds you must be the same as Christ Jesus: His state was divine, yet he did not cling to his equality with God but emptied himself to assume the condition of a slave, and became as men are; and being as all men are, he was humbler yet, even to accepting death, death on a cross. But God raised him high and gave him the name which is above all other names so that *all beings* in the heavens, on earth and in the underworld, *should bend the knee* at the name of Jesus and that every tongue should acclaim Jesus Christ as Lord, to the glory of God the Father (Phil. 2:5-12).

Perhaps it is not too academic a statement to say that the stress should be on "acceptance" rather than on "cross." Granted that death on the cross was most painful and the most repulsive form of death in the world of Christ's time, still it seems that we should stress his obedience. Obedience is the key to Christ's priesthood. Paul mentions the cross to show to what lengths Christ carried his obedience, but it was obedience that made his sacrifice acceptable to the Father.

Bulls' blood and goats' blood are useless for taking away sins, and this is what he [Christ] said, on coming into the world: *You who wanted no sacrifice or oblation, prepared a body for me. You took no pleasure in holocausts or sacrifices for sin; then I said, just as I was commanded in the scroll of the book, "God, here I am! I am coming to obey your will."* Notice that he says first: *You did not want* what the Law lays down as the things to be offered, that is: *the sacrifices, the oblations, the holocausts and the sacrifices for sin,* and *you took no pleasure* in them; and then he says: *Here I am! I am coming to obey your will.* He is abolishing the first sort to replace it with the second. And this *will* was for us to be made holy by the *offering* of his *body* made once and for all by Jesus Christ (Heb. 10:4-10).

It is certainly true that the death on the cross is a compelling example of Christ's obedience to the will of his Father. But the death of Christ has been allowed, in western theology, to overshadow and to even dominate our notion of Christ's priestly life. Christ's obedience was no less shown in any other phase of his life, even in his conception. He was obedient in Bethlehem, at Nazareth, and along each step of his public ministry. It is true that his understanding of his priestly life grew, and in this respect his obedience became more humanly perfect. It is true that he was freer as this understanding developed and that the conscious acceptance of death, of a cruel and contemptible death, was a superb act of obedience to the Father's will. There can be no belittling of this surrender of life itself.

But if death was a magnificent conscious surrender to the Father's will, so was the resurrection and so was the ascension. In fact, it would seem that there would be a more conscious awareness of the total scope of the Father's will in the light of his risen life. The point, and the only point, to be made here is that we must not overstress the importance of Christ's death when we are considering his priesthood. We must realize that all phases of Christ's life are of value in the attempt to penetrate the mystery of Christ's priesthood. This is of great importance when we come to a consideration of the Christian priesthood since this priesthood must be a faithful representation of that of Christ. Therefore, in a further consideration of Christ's priesthood an attempt will be made to consider all of Christ's life, and this includes his risen life.

We have seen so far that Christ is substantially priest. We explained that this means that "to be Christ" means "to be priest." Christ is by his very life the priest of the new covenant. We have seen, finally, that the key to the priesthood of Christ is his submission to the will of the Father. These are the general outlines of a consideration of the priestly life of Christ, which will be studied in greater detail. We shall use for the basis of this study the description of Christ as sanctifier, prophet, and king. In these three broad categories we shall be able to sum up the mediatorial role of Christ in his mission of restoring all things to his Father.

CHRIST AS SANCTIFIER

Part of the mission of Christ was to make men and all creation holy. He came to set creation back on the path to the Father, to consecrate it in love to the Father. Christ came on earth that men may have life and have it more abundantly. His task was to raise men to the dignity of sons of God so that they might share in the inner life of the Triune God and have the Triune God dwell with them.

I pray not only for these [the Apostles], but for those also who through their words will believe in me. May they all be one. Father, may they be one in us, as you are in me and I am in you, so that the world may believe it was you who sent me. I have given them the glory you gave to me, that they may be one as we are one. With me in them and you in me, may they be so completely one that the world will realise that it was you who sent me and that I have loved them as much as you loved me. Father, I want those you have given me to be with me where I am, so that they may always see the glory you have given me because you loved me before the foundation of the world. Father, Righteous One, the world has not known you, but I have known you, and these have known that you have sent me. I have made your name known to them and will continue to make it known, so that the love with which you loved me may be in them, and so that I may be in them (Jn. 17:20-26).

This, then, is the mission of sanctification involved in Christ's priesthood: "Father, may they be one in us, as you are in me and I am in you, so that the world may believe it was you who sent me." Christ is Son of God and dwells in filial union with the Father. So, too, in Christ, we are to dwell in filial union with the Father. Men are to be raised to the dignity of sonship, to a state in which they dwell in God and God dwells in them. This is not just some pious statement. Paul's letters are filled with statements relating to our sonship. We must never consider our sonship as a metaphor. It is, if we can believe Paul, the actual state of things in the new order.

Our sonship is from the Father through the life of Christ in whom we are made sons. In sharing his sonship we become partners in the inner love-life of the Trinity.

So far then we have seen that, through our Lord Jesus Christ, by faith we are judged righteous and at peace with God, since it is by faith and through Jesus that we have entered this state of grace in which we can boast about looking forward to God's glory. . . . but what proves that God loves us is that Christ died for us while we were still sinners. Having died to make us righteous, is it likely that he would now fail to save us from God's anger? When we were reconciled to God by the death of his Son, we were still enemies; now that we have been reconciled, surely we may count on being saved by the life of his Son? Not merely because we have been reconciled but because we are filled with joyful trust in God, through our Lord Jesus Christ, through whom we have already gained our reconciliation (Rom. 5:1-2; 8-11).

Christ's priestly life was directed then to the salvation and sanctification of men. Just as divinity was imposed on creation through the enfleshment of Christ, so divinity is to continue to be imposed on creation through the divinization of those who believe in Christ. The sanctification of creation is to be accomplished through the enfleshment of Christ and through its consequence, the divinization of men. It must be noted that this divinization of men is nothing more or less than their introduction into the divine life as sons. And it is all of creation, as Paul tells us, that is waiting with eager longing for the advent of the sons of God.

To accomplish this priestly work, Christ was enfleshed, lived, died, and rose from the dead. For men to become sons of God, they had to be freed from the bondage of sin. Men, as Paul mentioned, first had to be reconciled to God. The first step in this reconciliation was the overcoming of the "prince of this world." To establish the kingdom of God, the kingdom which belongs to reconciled men who are coheirs with himself, Christ first had to break the power of Satan over creation. Although this aspect of Christ's priesthood will be considered more in detail under the aspect of ruling the people of God, we introduce it here since man, before he could be reconciled to God, had to be freed from sin. Christ, to achieve this domination over Satan, lived a life of total obedience to the will of the Father.

Christ's role as sanctifier is found primarily in this obedience to the Father. This obedience kept him in Nazareth until he had reached maturity, and it moved him from this small village into the larger sphere of his public life, to the conflict with the religious leaders of the Jewish people, to his conscious acceptance of the Father's will as it led him to death, resurrection, and finally to exaltation at the right hand of the Father. It was Christ's obedience that overcame the disobedience of Adam. It was Christ's submission to the will of the Father that brought to the human race a super-abundance of God's favor.

Adam was created a steward over nature through his human awareness and his self-consciousness. He was the crown of material creation in that in him God had unified spirit with matter. His disobedience to the will of God resulted in an abundance of woe for all his descendants. But in Christ, the Father unified spirit and matter with divinity, and the obedience of Christ to the Father's will more than restored mankind to the favor of God. Christ's obedience opened to man not the opportunity to be God's acquaintance but the opportunity to be incorporated into the very life of God. Christ's obedience gave man the possibility of becoming a sharer in the divine nature. Paul writes,

Well then, sin *entered the world* through one man, and through sin death, and thus death has spread through the whole human race because everyone has sinned. Sin existed in the world long before the Law was given. There was no law and so no one could be accused of the sin of "law-breaking", yet death reigned over all from Adam to Moses, even though their sin, unlike that of Adam, was not a matter of breaking a law. Adam prefigured the One to come, but the gift itself considerably outweighed the fall. If it is certain that through one man's fall so many died, it is even more certain that divine grace, coming through the one man, Jesus Christ, came to so many as an abundant free gift. The results of the gift also outweigh the results of one man's sin: for after one single fall came judgement with a verdict of condemnation, now after many falls comes grace with its verdict of acquittal. If it is certain that death reigned over everyone as the consequence of one man's fall, it is even more certain that one man, Jesus Christ, will cause everyone to reign in life who receives the free gift that he does not deserve, of being made righteous. Again, as one man's fall brought condemnation on everyone, so the good act of one man brings everyone life and makes them justified. As by one man's disobedience many were made sinners, so by one man's obedience many will be made righteous (Rom. 5:12-19).

We see, from these words of Paul, that the second Adam, Christ, far more powerfully affected man through obedience to the Father than the first Adam had affected man by his disobedience. This is as it should have been. Christ, in virtue of his divinity united to his humanity, was certainly in a position to affect mankind more positively for good than Adam could possibly have affected mankind for evil. We have noted that Christ's obedience was the key to the reparation of man's past. But the offsetting of Adam's sin, as is clear from the Epistle to the Romans, was only a part of Christ's sanctifying role. Christ did more than restore man to the dignity that he had before Adam's sin.

Christ through his incarnate life of obedience had opened to man a life of sonship and of sharing the nature of God, a life that could never have been man's otherwise. It is in our adoption as sons that God shows us the full destiny that is to be ours if we dwell in obedient self-surrender in love to the Father. This destiny is ours through the self-surrender of Christ in filial devotion to the will of his Father. This is the aspect of Christ's priestly life with which we are most familiar.

There is also another element of the sanctifying role of Christ that we must consider. The mission of the Spirit is in reality a part of the sanctifying mission of Christ. Our sanctification is in reality our growth in the love of God. It is God's love for us and it is shown in our response in love. That the Spirit plays a part in this sanctification is clear from scripture.

Your interests, however, are not in the unspiritual, but in the spiritual, since the Spirit of God has made his home in you. In fact, unless you possessed the Spirit of Christ you would not belong to him. Though your body may be dead it is because of sin, but if Christ is in you then your spirit is life itself because you have been justified; and if the Spirit of him who raised Jesus from the dead is living in you, then he who raised Jesus from the dead will give life to your own mortal bodies through his Spirit living in you. . . . Everyone moved by the Spirit is a son of God. The spirit you received is not the spirit of slaves bringing fear into your lives again; it is the spirit of sons, and it makes us cry out, "Abba, Father!" The Spirit himself and our spirit bear united witness that we are children of God. And if we are children we are heirs as well: heirs of God and coheirs with Christ, sharing his sufferings so as to share his glory (Rom. 8:9-11; 14-17).

We shall consider the mission of the Spirit in greater detail later on since his mission is intimately connected with that of the Church. But we mention it here because it is a fruit of Christ's priestly activity. As Christ told the apostles at the Last Supper, "Still, I must tell you the truth: it is for your own good that I am going because unless I go, the Advocate will not come to you; but if I do go, I will send him to you" (Jn. 16:7).

The mission of the Spirit is to continue Christ's mission of sanctification and, as we shall see later, of prophecy and of ruling; his mission is the completion of Christ's priestly work. Christ continues his priestly activity in the world now and in the future through the mission of the Spirit who is with us. We shall have to consider this aspect of Christ's priesthood in detail since the mission of the Spirit plays a very important role in the priesthood as found in the Church. We must now consider the prophetic and ruling roles of Christ's priesthood in an attempt to synthesize them into our view of the total priesthood of Christ.

CHRIST AS PROPHET

In addition to Christ's sanctifying activity we must look to his role as the prophet of the new covenant. Prophecy, as used in the scripture, means the proclamation of the word of God. It does not necessarily look to future events, though it might. It is the revelation of God's will for men and it is primarily concerned with the present. The prophet in both Testaments is concerned chiefly with God's present will for men and attempts to persuade men to respond to the divine initiative. It is a proclamation of the wonderful works of God. Christ came to reveal to men the will of the Father and to show men what their response to God should be. This, too, as a part of the mission of Christ, cannot be divorced from Christ's priesthood, since Christ by his very life is a priest.

Part of Christ's mission was the revelation of the Father and of the Father's will. "At various times in the past and in various different ways, God spoke to our ancestors through the prophets; but in our own time, the last days, he has spoken to us through his Son, the Son that he has appointed to inherit everything and through whom he made everything there is" (Heb. 1:1-2). At the Last Supper, responding to Philip's request to see the Father, Christ answered, "To have seen me is to have seen the Father, so how can you say, 'Let us see the Father'? Do you not believe that I am in the Father and the Father is in me? The words I say to you I do not speak as from myself: it is the Father, living in me, who is doing this work" (Jn. 14:9-10).

Through the life of Christ, the Father revealed himself to us and gave us perfect insight into his secret purpose. That purpose was Christ himself and all that the incarnation has meant. It was the Father's purpose that men should come to him not as slaves or as acquaintances but as his sons. This purpose was revealed to us through the words and the life of the Son-made-man.

Christ is the prophet of the new Law and he is also the prophecy of the new Law. Christ not only proclaimed forgiveness of sins, his life on earth won that forgiveness for us. He not only proclaimed sonship, he was the Son. He not only proclaimed the future subjection of all things to the Father, he began this subjection through his life, death, and resurrection. He not only told men of the wonderful works of God, he himself was *the* most wonderful work of God. He not only spoke the words of God to men, he was the Word of God himself.

Christ, then, was the mystery that had lain hidden from all eternity in the bosom of the Father. His priesthood was concerned with revealing the will of the Father and of showing the world the wonderful saving love of the Father. In Christ is revealed the Father's concern for men and his saving will which freed men from bondage to sin and death. In and through Christ, he revealed his desire for the return of all things to himself. In Christ, he showed us his regard for all that is authentically human and his desire to divinize all that is truly human. God proclaimed through the incarnation that the world was not set for annihilation but that, through Christ, it was to be integrated with divinity for the everlasting destiny of sharing the glory of the Father himself.

In the Sermon on the Mount, Christ proclaimed the foundations of the new Law. His blood was a testimony to and a seal on the new covenant into which God had entered with man. His resurrection proclaimed the approval God had bestowed on the filial obedience of the Son and also showed to men the new life that would be theirs in the resurrection from the dead. The ascension into heaven, the exaltation of the incarnate Christ to the right hand of the Father in glory, revealed to man God's definitive and irrevocable acceptance of matter into his very being and showed man that all of creation had a destiny in Christ's life.

Christ, as priest, revealed in his words and in his life the will and design of the Father. This aspect of his priesthood is no less important than that one which concerns the sanctification of men, nor is it, in reality, separated from that aspect. Still, for purposes of attempting some description of the total priestly life of Christ, we have considered it apart from the role of sanctification, even though the very words of God have the power to make men new again. We must now come to the consideration of the third constituent of Christ's saving priesthood, that of ruler.

CHRIST AS RULER

The concept of Christ as the ruler has roots deep in the history of Israel. Moses ruled over the people in the desert after they had fled from Egypt, and this rule continued until his death on the borders of the Promised Land. This office of ruler then passed on to Joshua and was later fitfully taken up by the Judges who were sent to the people to save them from their enemies. This ruling function was finally assumed by the kings of Israel from the time of Saul until the conquest and destruction of Jerusalem. On the return of the Israelites from captivity in Babylon, the priests assumed the

office of ruling since the monarchy had come to an end during the exile. One thing that all of these various rulers of
Israel had in common was that none of them ruled in his
own name.

Israel, no matter what form of government it had, was
always a theocracy: God ruled over Israel as supreme Lord.
The kings and the other rulers were viceroys of God and
ruled in God's name. Yahweh, and Yahweh alone, was the
true ruler of this people. He was their God, and they were
his people. These earthly rulers of Israel were probably neither better nor worse than their contemporaries. But more
often than not they led the people astray toward false goals
and toward false gods. They directly or indirectly introduced
into Israel the culture of their pagan neighbors, and, as a
result, large segments of the people turned to idolatry. God
could no longer call his chosen people his own because they
had turned their backs on him and pursued foreign ways and
worshiped foreign gods.

Behind the whole notion of the covenant, both the old
covenant of Sinai and the new covenant that is Christ, is the
concept of God ruling over his people. This rule over the
people of God is an aspect of Christ's priesthood. He is our
leader in all things. But we must notice the difference here
between the two covenants. In the Old Testament, God
ruled in what we might call regal aloofness. It is true that he
dwelt among his people, but this dwelling among men was
in the context of majestic separation. It is not at all surpris-
ing that the rule of God among his people was likened to the
rule of their king.

In the New Testament, however, a much greater intimacy
is revealed. In the place of the metaphor of monarchy there

is the metaphor of the body. "Just as a human body, though it is made up of many parts, is a single unit because all these parts, though many, make one body, so it is with Christ. In the one Spirit we were all baptised, Jews as well as Greeks, slaves as well as citizens, and one Spirit was given to all of us to drink. . . . Now you together are Christ's body: but each of you is a different part of it" (1 Cor. 12:12-14; 27). In the letters to the Ephesians and to the Colossians, which are among the most theologically mature of Paul's letters, Paul completes the image: "*He* [the Father] *has put all things under his feet,* and made him, as the ruler of everything, the head of the Church; which is his body, the fullness of him who fills the whole creation" (Eph. 1:22). Again, "Now the Church is his body, he is its head. As he is the Beginning, he was the first to be born from the dead, so that he should be first in every way" (Col. 1:18).

This change of metaphor tells us many things. Undoubtedly, it expresses the fact that Christ is preeminent among the people of God. He rules as the head rules the body, but this rule is carried out, not in a tyrannical fashion, but in an intimate partnership with the members of the body. He is not a ruler who stands above his people but one who works closely with them to accomplish all that is to be done. The head is never separated from the body but is always active in promoting the well-being of the body. It does not dominate; it leads by its service to the lesser parts of the body. It directs the other parts but does not overwhelm them. It sets the goal and devises the means but it never tyrannizes.

Christ must, as ruler of the people of God, live among the people of God. Were he in any way separated from us, we could not survive as the people of God. But he rules us now as he ruled when he lived on earth—through service and love. He guides and teaches and moves, but in the gentle spirit of gift and of love, not in the harsh spirit of force. He tells us the goal of our lives and the goal of the people as a whole; he shows us the means, but he does not forcibly impose them on us. He helps us respond through his love which resides in us while, at the same time, he recognizes and fosters our responsible freedom.

Christ's is an intimate lordship over us because we are his brothers and sisters and because he respects our dignity and beauty as free sons of God. This does not mean that he does not place demands on us, even heavy demands. Christ's love can indeed be very demanding, the most demanding thing in the world. But it always remains love and consequently can be borne.

Christ as a priest is head, ruler, of the people of God. The establishment of the kingdom of God is the goal of his earthly mission, broader in scope than the mere forgiveness of sin. All of Christ's priestly activity looks to this and is directed to the complete reign of God over all things. It is for the establishment of God's rule in love that our sins are forgiven, that we are made sons, that we are accepted into the inner life of the Triune God. It is for the founding of the kingdom and for its growth that Christ became incarnate, lived on earth, died, was raised from the dead, and was exalted to the glory of the Father.

This is the ultimate design of the Father—the subjection of all things to Christ and ultimately to the Father. In a way, this aspect of Christ's priesthood sums up all the other aspects. Sanctification and revelation look to this setting up of the divine rule over all of creation. In this aspect of ruling all of the work of Christ is summed up. Thus, the rule of Christ is not confined to the ruling over the people of God. In his most mature thought Paul introduces a cosmic perspective into the establishment of the kingdom of God in and through Christ.

This you can tell from the strength of his [the Father's] power at work in Christ, when he used it to raise him from the dead and to make him sit at his right hand, in heaven, far above every Sovereignty, Authority, Power, or Domination, or any other name that can be named, not only in this age but also in the age to come. *He has put all things under his feet,* and made him, as the ruler of everything, the head of the Church; which is his body, the fullness of him who fills the whole creation (Eph. 1:19-22).

In this passage Paul identifies the Church as the Body of Christ and states that it can be called the fullness since it includes the whole new creation that shares in the cosmic rebirth under Christ, who is its ruler and head. This is the task that we have in Christ—to extend his rule to the whole of creation until that moment when, in his final priestly act, Christ returns to the Father all of creation. The full scope of Christ's priesthood is found in the establishment of the kingdom of God. Such a view opens up a cosmic vision of the priesthood that is quite compatible with Paul's most mature theology. Christ's mediatorial role looks ultimately to the submission of all creation to God.

The other aspects of Christ's priestly life, as sanctifier and revealer, seem to be subordinate to this ultimate goal. Sanctification, which includes the negative notion of the forgiveness of sin and the positive notion of the imparting of shared divine sonship, and prophecy look finally to the establishment and growth of the kingdom over which Christ continues to rule. The priesthood of Christ is, then, an extraordinarily rich reality and one that must include all that is authentically human. It must be found in all of creation, seeding it and nurturing it and bringing it to its ultimate divine fructification.

Christ in truly becoming man assumed all that is authentic in creation and integrated it with his divinity. This process still goes on since Christ's priesthood and his priestly activity continue even though he is in glory at the right hand of the Father. In heaven Christ remains the God-man and is still the priest of the new covenant. His priestly work is not finished because the kingdom has not grown to full stature. The continued growth of this kingdom requires for its success his continuing priestly activity. This present priestly activity of Christ is now found on earth in the priesthood of the people of God, the Church, Christ's prolongation in space and time. We must now come to a consideration of the Church and its mission. From these considerations we should be able to draw some conclusions about the priesthood of Christ as it is now to be found in the priesthood of the Church.

4. The Church

THE Church, as we have said several times already, is the prolongation of Christ in space and time. If this is true, the mission of the Church must be the same as the mission of the incarnate Son of God. It is also true that the priesthood of the Church must truly reflect the priesthood of Christ. Before going on to a consideration of the Christian priesthood in specific detail, it might be of value to look at the Church in terms of the mission of Christ.

We have already seen that the prime purpose of Christ during his life on earth was the establishment of the kingdom of God. It was to this goal that all his energies were directed. It was to this end that he lived in filial submission to the Father. For as Paul says, "The life and death of each of us has its influence on others; if we live, we live for the Lord; and if we die, we die for the Lord, so that alive or dead we belong to the Lord. This explains why Christ both died and came to life, it was so that he might be Lord of the dead and of the living" (Rom. 14:7-9). If then the goal of Christ was the establishment of the kingdom of God and if his priestly activity was directed to this goal, then the Church must foster the growth of the kingdom that Christ established.

The mission of the Church cannot differ from that of Christ. If Christ came to subject all things to the Father, then the Church must look to this subjection of all of creation as the complete expression of her mission. The kingdom was equated with the universe in Paul's discussion in the letters to the Ephesians and the Colossians. This hints at a cosmic mission for the Church. The Church, because it is involved in the growth of the kingdom, must be concerned with all of creation in a continuing effort to promote true human progress and to stimulate it on every level.

In some ways we have come to think of the Church primarily in juridical terms. We think of a distinction between laity and religious, between clerics and nonclerics. We think of it in terms of hierarchic structure—priests, bishops, and pope. We may possibly consider it as an organization which presents a closed body of truth to which believers must subscribe. The Church is often thought of in terms of buildings —churches, schools, and hospitals. All of these are aspects of the Church. Each one has a validity and each one is important, but to concentrate on them exclusively is obviously misleading.

In the western Church, possibly under the force of Roman legalism, the external structure of the Church has tended to overshadow to some extent other features of the Church. We, perhaps, have been somewhat deficient in our study of the mission of the Church. We must not allow the external structure of the Church to assume a greater importance than the mission of the Church. To illustrate the fact that we have overemphasized the hierarchic organization, canon law, and other such aspects, we need only recall the enthusiasm of Christians about the stress of Vatican II on the Church as the people of God.

The progressive domination of man over nature has created a situation of deep importance and with widespread ramifications for the Church. Man has slowly but surely begun the process of assuming prerogatives that once were thought to belong only to God. Some things have become so commonplace we hardly ever think of them, but they do show man's increasing mastery over nature. Flight is a good example.

Man has engaged in powered flight for only about sixty years and already has the technology to build commercial aircraft that will travel at three times the speed of sound and which will enable him to circle the earth in just a little more than half a day. We tend to forget that just twenty years ago we were impressed by a round-the-world flight that took over three days. Ten years ago the world was startled by the Russian success in sending aloft an artificial satellite. Now, even manned spacecrafts seem rather ordinary, although we still take an interest in space launches. We have close-up pictures of areas of the moon that startle us with their clarity and definition. We have photographs of Mars which also are extremely impressive.

In the sixty years since man first propelled himself through the air at a few miles per hour and over a distance of a few hundred feet we find ourselves poised for a leap into the unknown regions of outer space. We are only a few years from placing men on the moon, and men will probably explore the planets before the end of the century. All of this in one hundred years! Who in 1900 would have guessed that in 1970 men would walk on the moon? Who would have had the vision and the courage to express this vision even thirty years ago?

In medicine we have been able to drastically reduce infant mortality and to lengthen the average life-span by several years. A man of forty who is six feet tall is well above the average height of his generation, but he would not consider himself very tall in a group of average teen-agers. We have discovered drugs—wonder drugs we once called them —that rapidly control infection. We have invented artificial kidneys, artificial heart-pumps, pacers, and so many other devices for prolonging life and curing diseases that even a partial listing would consume pages in a book.

We have in this century seen whole new disciplines arise in the field of medicine and biology: microbiology, genetics, and many others. Scientists have probed deeper and deeper into the constituents of life and are aiming at the creation of life in the laboratory. In genetics the roles of DNA and RNA are under intense study and hold the promise (or, perhaps, the nightmare) of man's control of his future evolution. Should these dreams of man's control of human growth and heredity come true and should these opportunities be wisely used and carefully directed, to what unbelievable heights might man carry himself? Who can even guess at the progress of the next century if man gains and wisely utilizes these tremendous discoveries?

In his social life man has also seen tremendous changes in the last half-century. America entered World War I on a wave of patriotic enthusiasm that survived the cold and the mud and the degrading brutality of trench warfare but which failed to survive the postwar cultural upheaval. She entered World War II with the strength of righteous anger and with a strong will to avenge herself on those who attacked her. Korea was a strange unknown land in 1950 when Americans began to die there in battle. The nation never really mobilized, never fully applied herself to victory. Even then there was a vague, undefined feeling that war never really solves anything.

Perhaps the disillusionments of 1919 and 1945 were too strong for the country ever again to dedicate all her energies to killing. In 1944 and 1945 when whole cities were leveled in a phosphorous and magnesium holocaust, only a very few voices were raised against the mass destruction of modern war, and these voices were either unheard or were stifled. Now twenty years later there is no lack of voices to protest the accidental bombing of a small hamlet in Vietnam. Man's conscience has undoubtedly grown more delicate and sophisticated in matters concerning war.

Yet in other areas, even when respect for human life is concerned, man's conscience has become less delicate. Still, men as a whole manifest a greater concern for one another than they ever have before. It is a rare individual who does not at least know that most of the world is on the brink of starvation or at best living in conditions that are hardly compatible with human dignity. Man is greatly concerned with problems arising from human fertility, especially in those areas of the world least capable of supporting larger populations. Man, in general, is more sensitive to the conditions under which the majority of the human race is forced to live.

We could go on in other areas such as our growth in knowledge of the human mind, the emotions, and so forth. But it would seem that we have said enough. It should be clear that man has advanced with unprecedented rapidity during the last half-century. It should be equally clear that, barring nuclear catastrophe, man's material and even spir-

itual progress will continue to accelerate. The main question
for us is what this means to the Church. Does it, in fact,
have anything to do with the Church? The answer to this
question is an unequivocal yes. It would seem to flow from
the very nature of the Church that she be intensely concerned with man and his growth in control over nature. Let
us consider the Church in the context of modern human
progress.

The Church, as we have said, is the prolongation of Christ
on earth. She is the link set up by God between the human
and the divine. She is the seedbed of the divine in the
world. She is truly, in each of her members, the point of
insertion of the Triune God in the world, a world that has
been irrevocably accepted into a destiny in God. This destiny has been definitively revealed in the acceptance of the
universe into God through the bodily ascension of Christ
into glory. It is here that we have to apply the mission of
Christ to that of the Church.

Is the Church to be concerned only with the so-called
sacral ministry? Is her work completed with the offering of
the sacrifice of the Mass and with the dispensing of the sacraments? Is she to be contented with preaching the good
news of Christ's salvation, with Sunday sermons and religion
courses? Were she to confine herself to these ministries,
would she fulfill the totality of the mission entrusted to her
by Christ? These are basic questions, and the answer to
them will determine the Church's relation to the modern
world, really to the universe in general.

THE CHURCH'S ROLE OF SANCTIFICATION

There can be no doubt that those elements of the Church most directly oriented to sanctification and to the preaching of the word of God are extremely important. The Mass and the sacraments build up the people of God through a deepening union with Christ. The word of God orients them to their mission by explaining Christ's mission which has been entrusted to them. But the determining element in a growing understanding of the nature of the Church must be found in the nature of Christ's mission. We must continually look to the purpose of the incarnation if we are to understand the role of the Church in the history of man's salvific dialogue with God. Again, it is Paul who tells us what this role is.

Paul, in Ephesians, equates the Church with the cosmos, with the universe. This being true, the Church is irrevocably associated with the universe through man and through man's continuing attempt to gain total mastery over all of creation. The Church, if she is to be true to the mission of Christ, cannot either in word or fact dissociate herself from the world, from man's effort to control the universe. She cannot sit back and apodictically condemn or approve. She must show the world her interest, her sympathy, and her active participation in this dream of man. Let us look to this in greater detail in an attempt to gain some insight into the total mission of the Church.

Christ's mission of restoring all things to the Father cannot be divorced from man's progressive control of nature. Somehow or other these two movements must be blended, and the Church must be the agent of this mutual thrust forward. It must be the Church that transforms man's desire to shape the universe according to his own plan into the Father's design that all things be subjected to him in Christ. To stifle man's curiosity or to deaden his sense of beauty would not be proper and in the long run would be destructive both to man and to God's design. The Church must grow in the integration of the human and the divine in herself, in her understanding of the cosmic dimension of her mission, and in the holiness of her members—in their conscious integration of their humanity and the divinity they share in baptism.

The Church through her ministry of sanctification, through the liturgy, must foster the Christ-life of her members. She must always stress this union of the Christian with Christ as the foundation of the kingdom which she is struggling to build. The Church can never let this work of sanctification fall into oblivion. Rather, she must always attempt to make it deeper, more widespread, and more effective. This Christ-giving is always to be one of the most important tasks she has. It is of utmost urgency that she, in her members, grow in holiness, grow into a more vital union with Christ. Without this growth in Christ, without this conscious awareness that oneness with Christ is the goal of every Christian, she cannot fulfill the mission she has been given by Christ and which she exercises in the Spirit. This deepening of union with Christ is best accomplished through the sacrifice and sacraments that Christ has given to her.

The liturgical life of the Church is absolutely vital to the completion of the work that Christ has entrusted to her. The Church through her priests must always make these life-giving channels of divine life available to each of her members at all times. The work of sanctification, of conscious integration of the humanity and divinity of her members, will always be of prime concern to the Church, and hence to her priests. Sons of God must be raised up for the kingdom, and sons of God do not just spring up full grown. This christification of the members of the Body of Christ is not accidental but is rather the work of a lifetime for each member. It is to this deepening union of each Christian with Christ and, through this union with Christ, to the deepening union of all Christians with each other that the liturgical life of the Church is directed.

Sanctification, union with Christ, is the bond that holds the people of God together. The sanctification of each member dedicates the Body more deeply to the work of the kingdom. The deepening of the Christ-life in each member, if it is genuine, carries with it the deepening of the union of all the members with Christ. The deep inner union and devotion of the people of God is absolutely essential to the growth of the kingdom. The Church can never falter in this ministry of sanctification. Should she falter, the Bride of Christ could never lose the blemishes that would mar her beauty as she stands before her Bridegroom.

The Christian who fosters in a conscious way his union with Christ will feel impelled by the very force of this union to share it with others. He will be forced by the very dynamism of that love to give of himself to others, to share his time and his goods with those in need. He will find that this Christ-life in him will live only when he shares it with others, in love, in communal worship, and in all the multitude of activities in which he engages himself. The love of a Christian mother for her children will deepen the union with Christ that the children have. Since we are all members of the same Body, our strength in Christ will strengthen the Body and make each member stronger.

Our union with Christ will lead us into a deeper union with each other and give us a greater sharing in the power and love of Christ. The mutual sharing of the love of Christ that is ours will lead to mutual agreement and to a more effective mutual prayer life. "I tell you solemnly once again, if two of you on earth agree to ask anything at all, it will be granted to you by my Father in heaven. For where two or three meet in my name, I shall be there with them" (Mt. 18:19-20). Our union with each other in Christ and our sanctification of each other in Christ can only lead to the more effective fulfillment by the Church of her mission.

We do not and cannot live our Christian lives in some splendid isolation. Each Christian needs every other Christian. Each one of us has something to contribute to all the others and in so doing to the people of God as a whole. We have a duty to share Christ, to serve each other by giving Christ to one another. This receives its cultic expression in our communal worship. It receives expression in our way of dealing with each other in daily living. It is expressed in our mutual concern over family problems and family life, in our mutual effort to make our neighborhoods reflect more deeply the fact that Christ has redeemed the world. It is most fully expressed, perhaps, in the growing harmony that would result among all men if we were more conscious of the Christ-power that we possess and if we used that power to aid each other in our lives.

We do, indeed, need each other, and the human race would grow into deeper harmony and oneness of purpose if we all responded to our need for each other and for the

Christ we carry within us. We are, since we are sons of God, grace-making creatures and we can, so long as we are united to Christ, lead others to a deeper and more conscious union with Christ. This mutual strengthening and mutual love is part of the Church's mission of sanctification. If we do not fulfill this command of Christ to love and help each other, the Church cannot be fully successful in the mission that God has given her.

THE PROPHETIC ROLE

If the Church cannot falter in her task of dispensing the sacraments and in offering sacrifice, neither can she cease to preach the word of God "in season and out of season." She must importune, convince, exhort, and reprove. She must give the members of the Body the message of Christ, a message that stands for eternity as the revelation of the road of man back to God. This too is an element of the priesthood that can never be de-emphasized. The Christian must have Christ's message interpreted for him by the Spirit. This is not to say that he is only to sit and wait for the hierarchy to make a declaration to him on this matter. The understanding of the word and its preaching is incumbent on each member of the Church.

Christ's message as contained in the scriptures was given at a certain time, in a certain place, to people of a specific milieu and culture. These times, cultures, and places are foreign to us, and thus the full meaning of the scriptures is not always clear. The men who wrote the scriptures under the guidance of God never knew many of the problems faced by modern man. In fact, it would have been an anachronism for God to have given clear answers for problems of the twentieth or the thirtieth centuries to men of the first century. Although the message of the scriptures is Christ's message to men of the first century, the life-giving good news that God loved them and had redeemed them in Christ, this good news cannot be considered or understood apart from human culture in which it was originally given.

The totality of the Christ-event as contained in the scriptures must be studied continuously by the Church and continually reinterpreted by the Church for her members, for the people of God. The Church cannot survive in the twentieth century with a fourth-century understanding of Christ. To maintain that she could would be to deny that the Body of Christ is a dynamic, growing entity, and it would also be a denial of the revealing mission of the Spirit in the Church. It is one of the functions of the Spirit to help the Church come to the true meaning of Christ's message in the context of the twentieth century, or in whatever century she finds herself. This is merely to say that Christ's revelation was not a series of clear and distinct self-evident truths which are easily and readily applied to every and all circumstances.

The beauty and wisdom of the divine revelation is precisely that it is not a philosophy, facilely applied to every situation. Rather it contains God's mystery, and the Church must search this mystery for Christ's meaning to the contemporary world. We should not find it either strange or disconcerting to realize that Augustine's or Thomas' understanding of the scriptures and Christianity is inadequate to our situation. It would indeed be an anomaly if their understanding were adequate. If it were, their scriptural interpretation and theology would have been poor since they would have been divorced from their own milieu; therefore, they would have been quite meaningless to the people for whom they were written.

It should be clear that the message of Christ to the contemporary world must be studied deeply and prayerfully by every member of the Church, each according to his talent, training, and position. But the Church in the exercise of this aspect of her priesthood must rely on the prayerful reflection of each Christian on his situation in life. We must not presume that the revealing Spirit is active only in the theologian, the exegete, or the superiors in the hierarchy. We must rather assume that the Spirit is active in the whole Church, in each of the members to the degree that the Spirit wishes. It is to the whole Church the Spirit has been given, not just to some few members.

This fact in no sense denies the structured nature of the Church. We can assume with safety that the Spirit would be more active in those members of the Church to whom the government and growth of the Church have been entrusted in a special way, provided these members place no obstacles in the way of the Spirit. The assumption is valid, and we must presume the sincerity and ability of the shepherds of the flock until the contrary has been proved. Still, we cannot make the mistake of thinking that the Spirit is active only among certain groups in the Church. This would be a catastrophe! The preaching Church, under the watchful, loving guidance of the pastors, must search out the applications of the Christ-mystery to the contemporary situation. The pastors must apply themselves to a never-ending search into both the scriptures and tradition of the Church on the one hand, and into the contemporary situation of our culture on the other. This search demands patience, learning, honesty, and, above all, openness to the Spirit.

We cannot successfully meet the problems of the present by refusing to recognize the existence of the problems or by uncritically applying to them answers that may have been valid for the problems of the eighteenth or nineteenth centuries. Each Christian, responding to the Spirit in sincere love, must preach the message of Christ's love to others. The shepherds of the Church must preach the authentic message of Christ to the people of God, taking care not to merely repeat old formulas or timeworn solutions to problems that no longer exist. In other words, the preaching of the Church, while in continuity with the past and solidly based on the scriptures, must be contemporary. This is not an easy task, but when did Christ ever promise his Church ease and comfort?

THE CHURCH AS RULER

If the Church must never cease her work of sanctification and prophecy in the biblical sense of proclaiming the saving word of Christ, neither can she ever abandon her role as ruler. She must search into herself and into history and into all human disciplines to discover as best she can at any moment in what this ruling role consists. She must recognize first of all that any manifestation of triumphalism is out of place. She must recognize herself as the servant of man, not his tyrant. In this attitude of service she would only be imitating her Master "who came to serve and not to be served." She is here to lead all of mankind to God, but she cannot do this by lording it over man. She must draw, but she cannot overwhelm.

The Church must serve all the legitimate desires of humanity and expend herself in efforts to accomplish these desires. She must recognize that she must sanctify man without forgetting that she herself has not reached the fullness of holiness that is her goal. She must teach men the way to God while, at the same time, realizing that she is not the receptacle of all knowledge and is still engaged in searching out truth. She is, in a word, a pilgrim. This is the emphasis of Vatican II in its Constitution on the Church, an emphasis that is regrettably foreign to many Christians. She is still searching for answers, and even searching for the right questions. In short, just as she must grow in sanctification, she must also grow into her role as ruler of the universe, and even in her understanding of this role.

Christ, as we have already said, died and rose from the dead for the specific purpose of becoming the Lord of the living and the dead. Paul makes it clear, too, that this process of subjecting all things to the Father has not been completed. "For he [Christ] must be king *until he has put all his enemies under his feet*" (1 Cor. 15:25). This mission of Christ, still incomplete, has been entrusted to the Church, and this aspect of Christ's priesthood must be found in the priesthood of the Church. As we have already seen, the ruling aspect of Christ's priesthood is not confined to the juridical directing of the people of God. This is one phase of Christ's rule, but not the most important phase. Paul gives a cosmic perspective to the priesthood of Christ. The Church, as the divinely appointed agent involved in the perpetuation of Christ's priestly mission, must recognize the cosmic scope of her priesthood.

The Church has inherited the universe from Christ, and she must strive to understand its mystery and to incorporate that understanding into her christic vision of reality. She must concern herself with every method of penetrating into the mystery of creation, of matter, of spirit, and of man. Any science or discipline that explores these aspects of realities has much to contribute to the Church's understanding of creation, of man, of herself, and even of Christ. The Church must not only concern herself with these modes of man's progress, but she must actively support and encourage them. She must not fear them nor shy away from them. She must accept them as valid and encourage and actively promote them. She cannot allow herself to dominate them according to some preconceived notion of what is true and valid in creation and in the relationship of creation to God.

In a word, she must never again lose sight of the fact that she is a pilgrim, with a pilgrim's not-knowing. In this connection we might ask what a pilgrim is and what pilgrimage it is on which the Church is embarked. These are valid questions to be asked vis-à-vis the cosmic role of ruling that has been given to the Church by Christ.

THE PILGRIM CHURCH

Primarily, a pilgrim is a person on a journey. A pilgrim is usually defined as one who makes a long journey on foot to some specific place. Let us apply this definition to the Church. A long journey normally would imply the passing through unfamiliar terrain. Of necessity, the Church's whole journey to her goal, the new Jerusalem, is a passage through the unfamiliar and the strange. She has an ultimate goal that has been clearly specified but she has no detailed map of the route to be followed. She must find the way herself with the aid of the Spirit who is always with her.

As a pilgrim, the Church must study all the landmarks carefully and make human decisions on what road she must follow. At crossroads she must stop and carefully weigh the options open to her, and once the decision has been made, she must press on with vigor and courage. She must ponder each turn in the road and consult the compass which Christ has given her, the Spirit. The Church must travel on foot. This is not a journey filled with convenience and made in luxury. She must struggle over the rough ways in the road and climb over the obstacles that she finds in her way. There is no one who will clear them out of her way. She will not find luxury where she pauses briefly to rest nor should she expect to find herself in privileged and prosperous accommodations. This is not the mode of life proper to the pilgrim.

The Church should not expect to find herself welcome in all the places through which she must pass. She is a stranger in the country, and not all people take kindly to strangers. Yet she cannot afford to feel disdain for those who feel that the sun rises and sets on their own plot of ground. Struck or rebuked, she must find in herself the patience, the love, and the courage of a renewed attempt to serve even in the face of hostility. Stranger she must always be since her goal calls her elsewhere.

Still, she is never to be a stranger in the sense of refusing to try to understand the land through which she is passing. She may never be an alien in the sense of never striving to discover what is of value in the practices of those with whom she is dwelling. She can never stand aloof and refuse to reveal to the inhabitants the wisdom she has gained on her journey. Neither can she dogmatically dictate to them so-called universal truths which may or may not apply to present problems. She is still learning the way to her goal, and she must never forget this. She must of her nature be a stranger and yet, paradoxically, she can never be a stranger. Such is the nature of the pilgrim Church, struggling over rough and uncharted courses in her quest for her goal.

Nor can she cease to look at her goal. This is the light that draws her on, but it is not a clearly focused light. She has never seen the object of her quest. In a very real way, the Church must learn details of her goal from those she meets on her pilgrimage. Each civilization, each culture, and each man leaves some mark on her understanding of her goal. She learns, with every passing day, more about the beauty of the land toward which she is traveling. She can learn much or she can learn little—it is her choice. The scientific and technological culture can teach her a respect for matter that she had once but somehow has forgotten. This in turn will help her realize that heaven, her goal, will not be purely spiritual, that Christ, though no longer visible as he once was, is material. It will help the Church to realize that her goal is not the achievement of mere nirvana or an abode only suited to angels.

The Church must learn from everyone about everything. Learning, she must ponder and, under the guiding influence of the Holy Spirit, she must integrate all she has learned and incorporate it into her life and into her message. So, as a pilgrim she must struggle to learn her goal more clearly, to learn the way she must traverse to her goal. She must live in faith and in hope that the Spirit will never abandon her. She must show the tenderest possible compassion for those who journey along with her. She must never fear mistakes or fear to admit them, realizing that she is a pilgrim and that every pilgrim sometimes takes the wrong road. She is not confirmed in holiness nor is she exempt from failure. She is a pilgrim, and a pilgrim's course is difficult and beset by not-knowing.

The Church, as a pilgrim, exercises her priesthood in learning, in cooperating with all men in learning the secrets of God expressed in creation—in atoms and molecules, in life and in nonlife, in space and, above all, in man. She must ask questions of the culture in which she is, and she must, with the humility of the pilgrim, search out the answers. The Church must fulfill her priestly function of ruling man and the universe by putting herself at the service of man and of all creation. Only thus will she imitate her Master who came as the servant of all.

Man now is reaching for greater control of nature, and possibly now for the first time we can begin to believe that it is within man's reach to gain control over the universe and its processes. We can begin to gain a glimmer into a future of almost unimaginable fulfillment and growth. We can see man gaining for himself prerogatives once considered divine, and assuming a position in creation that was never before thought possible. This growth and progress is intimately re-lated to the Church's priesthood. In her priestly role she must direct this growth of man, and through her service to man she must subject all of this fruit of man's curiosity and creative sense of beauty to Christ.

The priesthood of the Church, as is evident, must reflect the priesthood of Christ. To do this the Church must engage in the offices which we have come to consider sacral. She must continue to offer sacrifice and administer the sacra-ments. It might be of some value to consider here that the sacraments themselves point to the ruling role of the priesthood, not merely with respect to the jurisdictional aspect but more especially with respect to the nature of the sacraments themselves. The sacraments are channels of God's saving love, vehicles through which God establishes our sonship, strengthens our union with Christ or reestablishes it should it have been lost. We must always keep in sight, though, that physical matter vivified by the Spirit has become the instrument of furthering Christ's kingdom and dominion over man and, through man, over all of nature. In every sacrament matter plays an absolutely indispensable role: water in baptism, oil in confirmation, bread and wine in the Eucharist, the spoken word in penance and matrimony, and so on.

The sacraments, then, are the expression of the new order of things, of Christ's incarnation: matter has been made sacred and has become an apt instrument for the divinization of man and of the cosmos. Moreover, the sacraments, as an expression of the new order of things, have as their goal a furthering and deepening of this new order, the order of the lordship of Christ the Priest. The new covenant is Christ, the God-man, the perfect union of the created and divine. Christ as a priest is also the exemplar of this new order that has been revealed in him. The goal of his kingly priesthood is the divinization of the entire cosmos and the completed union of creation with its creator.

The sacraments, while directed to personal growth in Christ, are not limited by this goal. Personal holiness, in fact, insofar as it is an expression of the priesthood of the Christian, must look to making all things new. Holiness in the biblical sense of the word means being set apart for some work of God. New Testament revelation has shown us the task assigned to each Christian by the Father. Each Christian is sent by the Father to carry on the work of Christ, the subjection of all of creation to the Father. Each one of us, by the fact of our having been baptized, is set apart for this task. Each one of us has the obligation and the opportunity of fulfilling in our own lives the priestly work of Christ.

The sacramental life of the Christian is an expression of his priesthood. This is just as true for the nonordained priest as it is for the ordained priest. It would be well to point out here an idea that will be developed at greater length later: the sacramental life of the Church is meaningless unless it involves the total Christian priesthood, the nonordained together with the ordained. Otherwise, the sacramental life of the Church would be severely and radically compartmentalized. The sacramental life of the Church demands the presence of the total Church.

The Christian, too, must realize that his prophetic role as priest also looks to the subjection of all things to the Father. The message we are to proclaim is the message of Christ crucified—but not only crucified. We must proclaim Christ crucified, Christ risen, and Christ ascended. We preach Christ, the Lord of the universe. This is the good news—not that God *was* once with us but that God *is* with us. We must both in word and in action clearly show the presence of God in twentieth-century life. It is not enough for the Christian of the present to say that the Church must lead man. He has to demonstrate it by his life. It is not enough to say that the Church is in sympathy with modern culture and sees good in it. He has to prove it in his life.

We must never forget that, just as Christ was once a pilgrim and just as the Church is now a pilgrim, each Christian is a pilgrim. Each one of us must live out our lives in not-knowing, just as the Church does. Each one of us must live in faith involved in a quest for something not clearly grasped. We must always remain strangers of sorts to all the multitudinous experiences of a lifetime. We must live out our days even partially a stranger to ourselves. We must attempt to integrate these experiences into a divinizing process and attempt to bring our partially integrated experiences into confrontation with all the aspects of reality with which we come into contact.

We are not a ship passing over water, leaving no lasting trace on our environment. Each of us shapes to a greater or lesser extent the fulfillment of creation. The mark we make on creation, whether for good or for bad, will never be entirely eradicated. We bear in ourselves the power and life of Christ. This power cannot go forth into the world without changing it. We can prevent Christ from penetrating that part of reality which is ours to influence, and if we do, all of reality will forever be impoverished. We can likewise struggle and suffer and bring Christ into our world, and that world, that part of the total creation, will become subject to the Father. In this way, our priesthood will have been exercised.

Still, we cannot expect it always and everywhere to be clear beyond doubt to what God is calling us. This we must discover each day. It is in the nature of a quest that the road is not straight or the path smooth. Each day should reveal to us something of God's growing love-union. In a true sense, each day should give a new orientation to our life in Christ. If we are serious about our Christianity, we should find it, generally speaking, a bit harder and a bit more demanding each day. I want to make clear that we are discussing the usual way in which God seems to work. In any individual case God may work out a man's goal and a man's relationship to himself in a different way. Each creature-Creator relationship is unique. But in the generality of cases, where we have data, it seems as if God becomes more and more demanding as the love-union grows.

The Christian caught up by the growing Christ finds a greater and greater need for faith and hope. It seems that the more closely we apply ourselves to searching out God's will for us in the context of the Church and our place in the culture of our society, the less sure we are of ourselves and the more we feel impelled to act contrary to "our better judgment." The more completely we devote ourselves to Christ, the more apparent becomes the risk-element of Christian faith. We may find ourselves confused, fearful, hesitant, doubting, and maybe even at times terrified. We may become like Peter walking on the water. He was alright until he realized what he was doing, and then he became confused and even scared. But we should not be surprised or upset at our confusion and doubt and fear.

We must not expect our lives and our growth in the sharing of the God-life to be different from the life-experience of the Church. She must grow and continually integrate new experiences into the growing God-consciousness that she is striving to develop. So too must each individual. As she is a pilgrim, so too are we. If we say that she must grow in holiness and in understanding of her mission and of her goal, continually reshaping and revising her understanding in the light of the Spirit and of the revelation of which she has been made the guardian, then we must expect to have to grow. And growth always implies tension. Were we perfect, there would be no need for growth.

It is our very imperfection, our not-knowing or not-doing, that can be the springboard to a closer and more vibrant love-relation with God. If we ever feel that we know, once and for all, the answers to all the questions about the goal we are pursuing and the way to get there, at that moment we have completely lost our way. God rarely, very rarely, reveals himself with that kind of clarity. Even were he to do so, the very revelation would demand a faith of rare strength and trust. On examination, it seems that the more forcefully God touches a person, the more clearly he lets himself be seen; the more audibly he speaks to a Christian, the more faith that person needs.

But what does all this say about our priesthood as Christians? One thing should be clear by now, our priesthood must be lived out in faith. Our priesthood should be a growing reality, a reality to be understood in terms of a growing dynamic awareness of revelation and of human progress. We must not allow ourselves to confine our vision of the priesthood to those things which we have, perhaps too narrowly, considered to be sacred. If we confine our notion of priesthood to the sacraments and to the sacrifice of the Mass, we have severely truncated the mission of Christ. We must never think that the sacramental life of the Christian is any more than a means to an end.

To understand the priesthood of the Christian we must understand the priesthood of Christ. It seems evident from the scriptures that the priesthood of Christ is directed to the subjection of all things to the Father. So too must be the priesthood of the Christian. All aspects of the Christian life should be oriented as means to this end. Any other view which would tend to make ends of those things which have been given to us as means would seem to be a distortion of the cosmic orientation of Christ's mission as it has been presented to us by St. Paul.

THE SACRAMENTS

Three of the sacraments are directed to the building up of the structure of the Church. It is through the sacraments of baptism, confirmation, and orders that the Church takes its form. It would be of value, it seems, to consider the Church in terms of these sacraments in general and then to treat each sacrament in particular to discover its relationship to the priesthood. It is not a new idea that the Christian priesthood is the result of three sacraments, not of one. However, in the past there has been a tendency in the western Church to think of holy orders as the sacrament which confers priestly power on the Christian. But in the light of the fuller notion of priesthood promulgated by Vatican II we must revitalize our theology of the total priesthood.

We have already considered the Church as the prolongation of Christ and the Church's mission as one of fulfilling and completing Christ's mission. This has important ramifications for our understanding of the sacraments of baptism, confirmation, and orders insofar as they touch on the Christian priesthood. Christ is the Son of God in human flesh. The early Councils of the Church tell us that he is consubstantial with the Father and consubstantial with us. By this they mean that he is of the same nature as the Father and that he is also man. The Church, as the prolongation of Christ, shares in both the divine and human aspects of Christ. The Spirit, too, has been sent to be the life-giving influence in the continued growth of Christ's kingdom. Therefore, the Church should sum up in a created and finite way the total activity of the Triune God. Let us examine this concept in a bit more detail.

We do not intend to go into a deep theological discussion of the inner life of the Trinity. We only wish to say that Christ is the Son of God, God of God, and Light of Light. The Son is related to the Father in a relation of filial love. This relation of the Father and the Son, the mutual love of the Father and the Son, is the Holy Spirit. We are only saying that Christ is a full, infinite member of the Trinitarian family and that these Three Persons are related to each other in a love-relation that is totally beyond our understanding, a love-relation in which the multiplicity of Persons reinforces the unity of nature.

We cannot discuss this topic at any length without coming to grips with the impenetrable mystery of the Trinity. Let us be content with saying that the Three Persons are related to each other in love. These love-relationships of the Three-who-are-One have been called the eternal processions in God. We shall use this terminology broadly. All we shall mean by it is that in God there are Three Persons engaged in an active, dynamic love-life. These eternal processions refer to the activity of God within himself.

There are other activities of God which are concerned with things outside of himself, activities such as creation, revelation, and redemption. The two of these that are of prime importance to our discussion are those which theologians call the temporal missions of the Son and the Spirit. These are the incarnation of the Son and the sending of the

Spirit to the Church on Pentecost. Thus, the total activity of God is summed up in the eternal processions and in the missions of the Son and the Spirit. We should expect that the Church, as the prolongation of Christ in time and space and as the Body of Christ animated by the life-giving Spirit, should sum up in herself the total activity of God. This sharing of God's total activity is, of course, a finite created summation of divine life and divine activity.

It should be clear that we do not intend to say that the Church is God. We are only saying that she shares in the divine activity in a created manner. We are not making any statements as to the mode of this sharing. We just wish to state that if the Church is to effectively carry on the work of Christ and if she is truly and effectively guided by the Spirit, she must somehow sum up in herself the activity of God. We shall say here in general that in baptism the individual Christian is given a new mode of being, that of being a son of God. As sons of God, if this is to be more than just a word, we share somehow in Christ's Sonship. We may call the Father "Father." We are in a real, though mysterious, way made partners in the love-relationship of the Father and the Son. As sons we share finitely with the Father and the Son in the spiration of the Holy Spirit. We become con-spirators of the life-giving Spirit of the Father and the Son.

We also wish to propose that confirmation is a sharing in the temporal mission of the Holy Spirit and that orders is a sharing in the temporal mission of the Son. Thus, in these three sacraments, through which the hierarchic Church is constituted, the Church would come to as full an expression as possible of God's saving activity. In such a scheme of things the other four sacraments would look to the strengthening and growth of the people of God completely formed through the sacraments of baptism, confirmation, and orders.

There has been a feeling in Christianity from very early times that these three latter sacraments were somehow quite different from the other four. It was this feeling which lead St. Augustine and other Church Fathers to develop the notion of a seal, a notion which grew into the concept of the sacramental character. This concept was more fully developed in medieval theology—the theory of a character or mark imprinted on the soul by these sacraments. Without going into any discussion of this theology we merely wish to indicate that even from the very early centuries of Christianity these three sacraments were considered as different.

We propose that these three sacraments are constitutive of the Church and that they are also three stages in the sacerdotal consecration of the Christian. What is proposed, then, is that the sacrament of orders is not the sole sacrament concerned with the Christian priesthood, but is merely the final step in the priestly consecration. All of these notions will now be considered in detail. We shall consider baptism, confirmation, and orders in themselves and then in their relationship to the total Christian priesthood.

These considerations should lead us to a better understanding of the relationship of the priesthood of the nonordained and of the ordained. We shall then consider the priesthood in its relationship to the world and to the final fulfillment of Christ's priestly mission of subjection of all creation to the Father. We shall attempt to focus this notion of the priesthood on the work of the Church in the twentieth century. We hope to be able in some degree to relate the priesthood to the prophetic call of Vatican II to bring the saving message of Christ to all of creation.

5. Baptism

THERE was one of the Pharisees called Nicodemus, a leading Jew, who came to Jesus by night and said, "Rabbi, we know that you are a teacher who comes from God; for no one could perform the signs you do unless God were with him." Jesus answered: "I tell you most solemnly, unless a man is born from above, he cannot see the kingdom of God." Nicodemus said, "How can a grown man be born? Can he go back into his mother's womb and be born again?" Jesus replied: "I tell you most solemnly, unless a man is born through water and the Spirit, he cannot enter the kingdom of God: what is born of the flesh is flesh; what is born of the Spirit is spirit. Do not be surprised when I say: You must be born from above. The wind blows wherever it pleases; you hear its sound, but you cannot tell where it comes from or where it is going. That is how it is with all who are born of the Spirit" (Jn. 3:1-8).

Baptism is our incorporation into Christ. It is at the same time the end of "living to the flesh" and the beginning of a life "lived according to the spirit." Baptism, the most necessary of the sacraments, looks to the past, insofar as it destroys our slavery to sin, and to the future, insofar as it constitutes us sons of God. Baptism has a twofold aspect which must be considered if we hope to understand the full priestly richness of this sacrament.

In him you have been circumcised, with a circumcision not per-formed by human hand, but by the complete stripping of your body of flesh. This is circumcision according to Christ. You have been buried with him, when you were baptised; and by baptism, too, you have been raised up with him through your belief in the power of God who raised him from the dead. You were dead because you were sinners and had not been circumcised: he has brought you to life with him, he has forgiven us all our sins (Col. 2:11-13).

Paul, in his letter to the Romans, states still more clearly this double aspect of the sacrament of baptism:

You have been taught that when we were baptised in Christ Jesus we were baptised in his death; in other words, when we were baptised we went into the tomb with him and joined him in death, so that as Christ was raised from the dead by the Father's glory, we too might live a new life. If in union with Christ we have imitated his death, we shall also imi-tate him in his resurrection. . . . But we believe that having died with Christ we shall return to life with him: Christ, as we know, having been raised from the dead will never die again. Death has no power over him any more. When he died, he died, once for all, to sin, so his life now is life with God; and in that way, you too must consider yourselves to be dead to sin but alive for God in Christ Jesus (Rom. 6:3-5; 8-11).

In Paul's view of salvation history man before baptism is a creature who is weak and perishable, a slave to the flesh. By this he means primarily that man is selfish, closed in on himself, and incapable of life in God. His horizons are totally circumscribed by his own limitations, and his vision of reality is never focused on anything beyond himself. He is one given to "fornication, gross indecency and sexual irresponsibility; idolatry and sorcery; feuds and wrangling, jealousy, bad temper and quarrels; disagreements, factions, envy; drunkenness, orgies and similar things" (Gal. 5:19-21).

In other places Paul says that such a man is a slave to his own appetites and to sin and is subject to death. Obviously, when saying an unbaptized man is subject to death, Paul is speaking of spiritual, or eternal, death. Such a man, encased in the armor of his own ego, is not open to God's love. For a time, before Christ, circumcision and faith in the covenant-promises of God justified a man. But with Christ's redeeming priesthood circumcision lost its meaning. Paul makes it clear that faith and baptism are the prerequisites for the forgiveness of sins and for incorporation into the new people of God. Baptism is necessary for men to become members of the family of God.

INCORPORATION INTO CHRIST

Before Christ, man could not approach the Father as a son. We see in the Old Testament many relationships between God and the men he chose to lead the Israelites. But never is there any hint of a true son-Father relationship. There is portrayed a relation of friendship, of greater or lesser intimacy, but never one in which a man could truly say *Abba*. A Hebrew would never have so addressed God, but from the New Testament we are told to call upon God in these terms

—in terms of familial love. In baptism a man is incorporated into the inner life of the Trinity, is made a member of the "Trinitarian family." It would be of value to examine, as best we can, this mysterious new state of things. Here, as elsewhere, let us turn to St. Paul.

Paul speaks in many places of our incorporation into Christ. He uses many different metaphors to describe this union with Christ that is effected in the waters of baptism. As we have already seen, Paul describes baptism in terms of dying, being buried, and rising with Christ; in general, he describes baptism as our sharing in the climactic salvific activity of Christ's life. Baptism is our real sharing in the most dramatic aspects of Christ's priestly mission. Paul speaks of being baptized into union with Christ, of being clothed with Christ and of being made heirs under the promise (Gal. 3:26-29). And, again, Paul says,

You have stripped off your old behaviour with your old self, and you have put on a new self which will progress towards true knowledge the more it is renewed in the image of its creator; and in that image there is no room for distinction between Greek and Jew, between the circumcised or the uncircumcised, or between barbarian and Scythian, slave and free man. There is only Christ: he is everything and he is in everything (Col. 3:9-11).

Paul uses several other descriptions such as the Body of Christ, the Temple of the Spirit, and so on. The expression, however, which recurs over and over again is "you are in union with Christ." Of this union with Christ, Paul makes some rather startling statements: "And for anyone who is in Christ, there is a new creation; the old creation has gone, and now the new one is here. It is all God's work. It was God who reconciled us to himself through Christ and gave us the work of handing on this reconciliation" (2 Cor. 5:17-18). "A spiritual man, on the other hand, is able to judge the value of everything, and his own value is not to be judged by other men. As scripture says: *Who can know the mind of the Lord, so who can teach him?* But we are those who have the mind of Christ" (1 Cor. 2:15-16).

These statements of Paul are indeed startling. It is obvious to anyone who has read all of St. Paul that he means what he says. Those in union with Christ, those who are baptized and live a life of faith, share Christ's life, his words, his thoughts, his desires, and his power. In baptism man partakes in the divine nature. In union with Christ, he has truly become a son of God. In Christ, who is by nature the Son of God, we become sons of God, but no less sons because adopted. We share the same sonship with Christ, though in a different way. By nature he is the infinite and uncreated Son. By adoption we are finite and created sons.

We have been really admitted into the inner life of the Trinity. We share in Christ's relation to the Father and we share in the love which the Father lavishes on the Son. Since we live in Christ and share in the being of him who is our new vital principle, we, together with Christ and the Father, share in the spiration of the Holy Spirit who proceeds from the Father and the Son. We become grace-making creatures. Truly, in an astounding and mysterious way, we have been caught up into the dynamism of Trinitarian life and love. We have become divine beings while never ceasing to remain men. We have achieved a likeness to God beyond the dreams of the author of the Book of Genesis.

These are hard concepts to grasp since they can be glimpsed only in the light of faith. When we look at ourselves, the number of whose days are so limited, how can we imagine that we share in the life of him whose days are without number? When we consider our limits and our weaknesses, how can we presume to say that we share in the power of him who created the universe, who sent forth from himself innumerable reflections of himself to fill the nameless void? When we look into the pettiness and ugliness of some of our human strivings, how can we say we share in the bounty and the beauty of him who is Lord?

Yet, Paul tells us that we do, that in baptism we have been raised with Christ to share his life, his power, and his beauty. We rise from the waters of baptism as creatures destined to share in the lordship of Christ over all things. Paul does not say that we are given the fullness of this sharing from the very fact of baptism. In fact, it should be clear that we do not fully share this from the beginning. This is what our lives as Christians are all about. We are meant to grow into this shared Trinitarian life, with our death as the moment of greatest growth. It seems as if our lives as Christians are a constant attempt at a conscious integration of our humanity with the divinity that is given us at baptism. We can never come to our full stature as Christians unless we are conscious of our power, our dignity, our love, and our life.

The love of God is a creative love, productive of the object of that love. When God loves, he creates the object of his love. This love shows itself in creation, in God's providence, in his redemptive life, death, and resurrection. Each of these manifestations is productive. They produce creatures of all kinds when they had not existed before; they produce sons of God when before they did not exist. This is the love we have to share.

As we grow into a deeper conscious union with Christ, this creative aspect of our life should become clearer to us. As we are more consciously aware of our union with Christ, we should see this creative love touching our families, our environment, and ultimately our culture. We should, since we are closer to Christ and possess him more fully, bring him more completely to all the people we know and to all of creation to which we apply ourselves. As we become more and more other Christs, Christ is more tangibly present to creation. We bear Christ's love in our being, and this love cannot leave others untouched. Our Christian life should bring good from evil, knowledge from ignorance, health from sickness, order from chaos. If we apply this love to our environment, and we must give it if we are to keep it, then it must be influential because it is Christ's love.

It seems that to a Christian there should be no philosophical problem of evil, considering evil in the broad sense of limitation and imperfection. This limitation, to a Christian, should be considered as one of God's greatest gifts to us. Because of limitation we can share in God's creativity; we can create, as was said above, good from evil, knowledge from ignorance, order from chaos. Were everything perfect, life on earth would be meaningless to a man and probably a rather boring state of affairs. How exciting would life be if we were never needed by anyone? What value would human existence have if there were no effort needed to improve the environment? How could we be happy if we never knew the spur of curiosity and the joy of discovery? What would beauty mean to us if there were no ugliness to respond to our hands and if there were no limitations to be extended and remodeled?

The Christian should not look at creation with an exasperation that brings despair. He cannot, while remaining a Christian, throw his hands in the air and quit the struggle. His love of creation, which love he shares with Christ, cannot allow him to quit even in the face of the enormity of the task confronting him. If the Christian does not bring the creative love of Christ to bear on the limitations of his environment, then that love will not be present and creation will forever be the poorer. But to most fully apply to creation the productive love of Christ in us, we must be aware of it. The life of a Christian must be one of conscious realization of Christ who dwells in us and in whom we dwell.

The Christian shares in all the powers of Christ. He, of course, shares in the priesthood of Christ, and this shared priesthood is expressed in the application of our "Christhood" to creation. The Christian priesthood, insofar as it is shared in baptism, is the application to creation of our sharing in the inner life of the Triune God. It is the sharing with others and with all of creation of the God-life that has become ours in baptism. In short, it is the application to and penetration of all of reality with the christic life, love, and power which we here received in baptism.

INCORPORATION INTO THE CHURCH

In baptism, as we have said, the individual Christian is caught up into the life of the Trinity. A wondrous change, but one seen only in faith, has occurred. A man has been adopted into the family life of God. But baptism is not merely an individual experience. It is the sacrament that incorporates a man into the people of God, into the Church. It is, in fact, the sacrament that builds the people of God, gives them their life. As the prolongation of Christ, the Church is completely oriented to fulfill and complete the mission of Christ. As an extension of the Incarnate Christ in time and space, the Church is charged with the continuing work of the integration of all things into Christ.

When Christ ascended into heaven and took his seat in glory at the right hand of the Father, matter, in the person of Christ, was accepted into the inner life of God. God put his final and definitive seal of acceptance on creation and showed us at the same time his desire to incorporate all of creation into himself in and through Christ. This was the goal to which Christ's priesthood had been directed. In the moment of the ascension the priesthood of Christ reached its first fulfillment—creation had been radically saved and reduced in love to the Father's will. But this work, though assured of completion in Christ's bodily return to the Father, was not yet fully matured nor fully accomplished. This task was left to the Church, and to the Church's priesthood, to be carried on to total fruition under the guidance of the Spirit.

In a very real sense the Church is herself the priesthood of Christ continued through all ages. This priesthood, this setting up of what St. Peter calls "a chosen race, a royal priesthood," is accomplished in baptism. In reality, baptism is the first priestly sacrament, the sacrament which establishes the priestly people of God. And this priestly people from its very inception is charged with the completion of the sacerdotal mission of Christ—to effect his lordship over all of creation.

The Church is the priestly milieu into which each Christian is received as he rises from the waters of baptism.
His Christian life is not, and can never be, an individualis-
tic approach to God. In baptism he has been incorporated into the people of God, and his growth in Christ is
intimately linked to the growth of the people of God in
Christ. The mission of the individual Christian is inseparable
from the mission of the Church.

The people of God, the Church, is not a static, once-and-
for-all organization. She must be dynamic and growing. Nor
is her growth confined to an increase of numbers or of influence or to a growing geographical distribution. Each of
these is important, but the growth of prime importance for
the Church is a deeper and deeper penetration into the mystery of her own role in the christification of all things. This is
not a simple task, nor is it one that will be completed before
Christ returns to us again in the flesh—before the parousia.

In this growth the Church must walk in faith, as a pilgrim.
But where is she to learn her role? Would it not seem right
that she learn it from the life-struggle of every man? God is
not going to give this understanding to her fully articulated
and completely clear. The moment that the people of God
see their role in creation with complete clarity and for all
times and conditions, at this moment the Church can be
certain of one thing—the parousia has come, and Christ is
with us once again on earth.

RESPONSIBILITY FOR GROWTH

One of the most important aspects of the Christian priesthood, as established through baptism, is the growth of the

Body of Christ. This growth must be found at all levels and in every aspect of the Church. Growth in holiness, growth in understanding, growth in prophecy in the biblical sense of proclamation of the saving work of God, growth also in numbers and in influence—all these must be found. And all of these areas of growth are the responsibility of each Christian. For too long have the vast majority of Christians been conditioned to leave the responsibility for growth to the few who have been granted authority over them. This has, sadly, led to a stratification in the growth of the Church.

We have too long taken Paul's image of the Church as the Body of Christ in a completely mechanistic sense—as if to say "I am only a foot or an arm, what can I do to help? Let's leave that to the head." This is an abdication of Christian responsibility. Each Christian, no matter how poorly educated, no matter how inarticulate, no matter from what rank of society, has a definite and important contribution to make to the growth of the people of God. Each one of us confronts God in faith in the situations of daily life. The experiences with God that each one of us gains in our living out the Christian life are of unique value to the Church. There is nothing in the scriptures to suggest that the living Spirit who animates the Church confines himself to the pastors. If we want an example, we need only look at Catherine of Sienna whose influence over the pope ended the stay of the papacy at Avignon.

Of course, examples of authentic workings of the Spirit in the ranks of the faithful could be extended almost without end. But we tend to say, "Well, they were saints and we are not." Is this more than rationalization? Were these people in the beginning of their work any different from the rest of us?

The difference, if there is one, is only one of degree. It is true that God has given extremely great graces to some few in the history of the Church. But this in no way implies that the graces applied to each Christian are unimportant.

A charism is a grace given to someone to accomplish a specific mission in the Church. We have absolutely no reason to believe that charisms are limited to bishops or to priests or to religious. In fact, as Vatican II declared, we have every reason to believe that this is not the case:

It is not only through the sacraments and Church ministries that the same Holy Spirit sanctifies and leads the People of God and enriches it with virtues. Allotting His gifts "to everyone according as he will" (1 Cor. 12:11), He distributes special graces among the faithful of every rank. By these gifts He makes them fit and ready to undertake the various tasks or offices advantageous for the renewal and upbuilding of the Church, according to the words of the Apostle: "The manifestation of the Spirit is given to everyone for profit" (1 Cor. 12:7). These charismatic gifts, whether they be the most outstanding or the more simple and widely diffused, are to be received with thanksgiving and consolation, for they are exceedingly suitable and useful for the needs of the Church (Constitution on the Church, Chapter II, Number 12).

In virtue of our baptism, each one of us has been incorporated into the love-life of the Triune God. Each one of us is a God-bearing creature. In each one of us the Father, the Son, and the Spirit have come to dwell. The same Spirit that animates the Church animates each Christian. It would, indeed, be a very strange state of affairs if the Spirit were productive only in the few who have been given some degree of authority over the people of God. It is a denial, in fact, of the priestly office received in baptism to refuse to accept in faith the Spirit-directedness of each Christian. The Spirit moves each of us and aids each of us in finding the authentic Christian life.

For too long a time we have, as ordinary Christians, been accustomed to feeling that the Church gives Christ to us, without reflecting on the fact that we must give Christ to the Church also. If in virtue of our baptism we are truly Christ-bearers, then we truly have the opportunity, the ability, and the obligation to bring Christ to the Church. This notion should in no way seem strange to us. Vatican II tells us in no uncertain terms that the Church has not reached, nor will reach for a very long period, her full perfection in Christ. It is the priestly duty of each one of us to contribute to the Church's growth in holiness, in the understanding of her mission, and in her priestly life. We must never for an instant think that our Christ-life and Christ-understanding is unimportant to the pilgrim Church as she struggles to grow into her mission. The Church's mission of the return of all things in Christ to the Father is dependent for its success on each member of the people of God.

To be as complete, and therefore as successful, as possible, the Church's approach to the world must encompass the life-experience of each member of the total Church. The Church was never meant to be an organization in which the few in power decreed and in which the rest showed unquestioning and unthinking obedience. This would be a slavery to replace what Paul calls the slavery to the Law from which we were delivered in Christ. If we are to be full members of the kingdom of God, we must be active in all the dynamics of the growth of this kingdom. The Spirit apportions himself and his gifts to our abilities, our training, and the problems and situations that we meet.

If we lead a thoughtful and productive Christian life in cooperation with the Spirit who dwells within us, then our growth in the understanding of the workings of the Spirit in us is of great importance to the Church. Only from the experiences of each of us can the Church gain a true perspective of the Spirit's desires for the Church. This articulation of our life-experience to the Church is no small part of our priestly baptismal mission. We shall treat this in our discussion of confirmation.

THE BAPTISMAL PRIESTHOOD

From our baptism we become priests, sharing in the priesthood of Christ. Our baptismal priesthood looks to the world and it looks also to the Church. It contains the triple aspect of Christ's priesthood; it looks to sanctification, to prophecy in the biblical sense, and to ruling through love expressed in service. Each of these roles has a personal and a community aspect. Sanctification as a priestly office looks to our own sanctification and to that of the community and, ultimately, to those who are not yet members of the community of salvation. Prophecy looks to our own understanding of the wonderful work of God that we have become. It reveals to us our dignity, the dignity of sonship that we have received in baptism. It proclaims to us our responsibility of preserving and increasing this dignity.

We must also let the Church, for her edification and growth, see what a miracle of God's love we are. She must be allowed to share in the saving love that God has shown us. She must be given the opportunity of growing in the Spirit by her awareness of the Spirit's activity in each of us. And, finally, the universe which still stands beyond the community must see in us God's saving designs. We must proclaim the Christ who has risen and who is still striving to capture the love of all creation so that in the end God is all in all. We must, too, rule ourselves in response to the yoke and the burden of Christ, the yoke that is gentle and the burden that is light. We must gain mastery over those elements in our personality and character that keep us from true growth in Christ. We must share in the ruling of the Church, which is our community, and we must give ourselves also to the growth of the Church's mastery, through service, over all of God's creation.

Since we may have, in view of our background and of the context of the theological development of the past several centuries, an inadequate notion of the ruling function of the Christian priesthood, we wish to stress again that by ruling we mean service. We must serve our own growth in Christ. We must serve the Church, and in this service we must serve all of creation. The whole people of God must serve the community so that it may grow in holiness and responsiveness to the Spirit. And the Church must also be found serving all the legitimate needs of mankind and promoting all authentic human values. This is the expression of Christ's priestly role as the ruler of all things.

God's designs look toward the growth of all the potential that he has lavished upon creation. This growth requires the loving care of the Church and demands heroic effort on the part of the people of God as a whole and of each individual

Christian. Only when we realize that we are here to serve and to foster and protect all authentic human progress, only then can we adequately fulfill the priestly activity of ruling. This also is a theme to which we shall return later.

We shall summarize this by recalling that in baptism we have become sharers in Christ. We have become "Christs," sharers in Christ's life, power, and being. Christ was by his nature a priest, the Priest. In sharing in his life we automatically share in his priesthood and his priestly activity. Insofar as we are Christians, insofar as we share Christ's life, we are priests. Every aspect of our Christian life is an aspect of our Christian priesthood. Everything that contributes to our growth in Christian living also contributes to the deepening and strengthening of our priestly activity. Every life-situation that challenges our Christianity is also a challenge to our priesthood.

Quite simply, we are saying that to be a Christian means to be a priest. Our priesthood, received in baptism, is our Christianity. A Christian is a priest, a member of a priestly people. Every true act of a Christian is a priestly act. This statement will require greater specification as we proceed in the development of these thoughts on the priesthood.

It must be stressed that the totality of Christian priesthood is not expressed sacramentally in baptism, but then, the totality of Christian life is not expressed in baptism either. This sacrament is but the birth of the Christian. It is the beginning, the initiation, of the Christian life. It was stated before that we must consciously integrate our humanity with the divinity that we have shared in baptism. So, too, we must become consciously aware of the priestly role that has begun in the waters of baptism, and we must become more completely developed priests through the other sacraments. Baptism brings us into the family life of the Trinity. But this is just the beginning of our priestly commitment also. Baptism is the sacrament of our sharing in the eternal processions of the Trinity; through it we are really incorporated into the life of God. This sharing is the foundation of our priestly life and our priestly activity.

Christ became the Priest of the new covenant at the moment of his incarnation, at the moment of his taking on flesh. We became priests at the moment of baptism, at the instant when our humanity took on the richness of divinity. Christ was a priest in every activity he performed. We, too, are priests in every act that is compatible with the Christ-life in which we share. Every act that strengthens our union with Christ is a priestly act. It would seem strange if this were not so. Even the most trivial act of a Christian is an act that can unite us more consciously with God. We are accustomed to think, perhaps, that only the activity with major consequences in our lives should be dignified with the name Christian. But this does not make any sense. Once we are in union with Christ, everything we do, we do as "another Christ."

This christic aspect of our lives is not something that is turned on or off for some specific set of activities, such as going to Mass, receiving the sacraments, or praying. This would be to say that we are Christians only at those times, and Christ fulfills the role as the vital principle of our lives only at those times. Were this true, our Christ-life would be at best an intermittent thing, coming or going merely on the basis of some norm external to our lives. This would be extremely difficult to accept. In fact, it makes no sense at all.

Our Christianity remains with us at all times and pervades the totality of our lives provided we have not destroyed the union with Christ that we have received in baptism. So long as we remain united to Christ, so long as we remain God's sons, every activity we perform deepens Christ's hold on us.

This is true of our priestly life also. If we are united to Christ, the Triune God dwells with us, and through us brings his saving power to bear on every aspect of reality with which we come into contact. We need a deep faith to realize this, but it is true. Every activity of ours is an activity of God also and is an application of Christ's priestly power to the world. Our baptismal ordination to the priesthood sets up a life that is totally priestly and totally directed to the return of all things to the Father in Christ. No activity is too insignificant or too "worldly" to escape this christifying power. Only sin escapes this cristification.

The priesthood of the Christian, then, looks to the christification of all reality, not just to those things in our lives which we designate as religious. This is an extremely important notion if we are to live out our priesthood in its completeness. We must continually strive to grow more deeply aware of our baptismal commitment and in faith attempt to live out this mission consciously, in this way bringing to bear on reality the power of Christ which has been entrusted to us as sons of God. The growth of the kingdom is the responsibility of each one of us. This growth will be better effected if we are conscious of the full dimension of our priestly life in Christ.

6. Confirmation

WE have discussed baptism as the sacrament that gives to man a share in the eternal life of the Triune God. It is the sacrament that raises man to the dignity of a son of God. It introduces him into a priestly community and bestows on him both the opportunity and obligation to be a priest, to be a chosen mediator between creation and God. We have also mentioned that confirmation may be considered as the sacramental sharing in the temporal mission of the Holy Spirit. In this chapter we shall discuss the mission of the Spirit in order to gain some understanding of it. Then we shall consider the Christian priesthood in the light of this understanding.

In my earlier work, Theophilus, I dealt with everything Jesus had done and taught from the beginning until the day he gave his instructions to the apostles he had chosen through the Holy Spirit, and was taken up to heaven. He had shown himself alive to them after his Passion by many demonstrations: for forty days he had continued to appear to them and tell them about the kingdom of God. When he had been at table with them, he told them not to leave Jerusalem, but to wait there for what the Father had promised. "It is" he had said "what you have heard me speak about: John baptised with water but you, not many days from now, will be baptised with the Holy Spirit." Now having met together, they asked him, "Lord, has the time come? Are you going to restore the kingdom to Israel?" He replied, "It is not for you to know times or dates that the Father has decided by his own authority, but you will receive power when the Holy Spirit comes on you, and then you will be my witnesses not only in Jerusalem but throughout Judaea and Samaria, and indeed to the ends of the earth" (Acts 1:1-8).

When Pentecost day came around, they had all met in one room, when suddenly they heard what sounded like a powerful wind from heaven, the noise of which filled the entire house in which they were sitting; and something appeared to them that seemed like tongues of fire; these separated and came to rest on the head of each of them. They were all filled with the Holy Spirit, and began to speak foreign languages as the Spirit gave them the gift of speech (Acts 2:1-4).

The Apostles were soon in the streets preaching the word of salvation. When the people in Jerusalem were startled, Peter explained to those standing about what had happened:

Then Peter stood up with the Eleven and addressed them in a loud voice: "Men of Judaea, and all you who live in Jerusalem, make no mistake about this, but listen carefully to what I say. . . . this is what the prophet spoke of: In the days to come—it is the Lord who speaks—I will pour out my spirit on all mankind. Their sons and daughters shall prophesy, your young men shall dream dreams. Even on my slaves, men and women, in those days, I will pour out my spirit" (Acts 2:14-18).

Pentecost Sunday, the day of the Harvest Festival, marked the beginning of the temporal mission of the Spirit. As was foretold by the prophet Joel, the new age would be the age of the Spirit, the time when the Spirit would dwell with men and direct their activity and give them power to be witnesses to Christ throughout the world. We live in the last days as described in scripture. The Spirit has been given to the Church and in confirmation has been imparted to each of us.

The pages of scripture, especially the writings of John and Paul, give us many indications of the works of the Spirit. We must study these passages while always keeping in mind the statement of St. Gregory Nazianzen that the Spirit and the work of the Spirit are still being revealed to us in the Church. With this admonition in mind let us look to the scriptures.

THE MISSION OF THE SPIRIT

At the Last Supper, Christ told his apostles,

And when he comes [the Spirit], he will show the world how wrong it was, about sin, and about who was in the right, and about judgement: about sin: proved by their refusal to believe in me; about who was in the right: proved by my going to the Father and your seeing me no more; about judgement: proved by the prince of this world being already condemned. I still have many things to say to you but they would be too much for you now. But when the Spirit of truth comes he will lead you to the complete truth, since he will not be speaking as from himself but will say only what he has learnt; and he will tell you of the things to come (Jn. 16:8-13).

Thus, John tells us the Spirit is sent to us to continue the revealing work of Christ and to lead us to a deepening understanding of the saving mission of Christ. It is in the light of the Spirit's activity and the Spirit's guidance that we come to a fuller understanding of Christ's work in the context of our own milieu. It is the task of the Spirit to enlighten us so that we do not attempt to live out in the twentieth century a first- or tenth- or fifteenth-century understanding of Christ. The Spirit continually re-presents to the Church the mission of Christ as relevant to the present time. The Spirit shows that the world was wrong about sin, uprightness, and judgment. It is important to realize here that John uses the word "world" in three distinct senses. Here he is speaking not of creation but of the enemies of Christ. He is speaking of all created reality that is subservient to the "prince of this world," Satan.

The Holy Spirit will, according to these words of John, appear in the role of a prosecutor. His words and actions will manifest the evil of the enemies of Christ and will also show their condemnation. The sin of the world was its refusal to believe in Jesus, and this sin will be made evident by the Spirit. The Paraclete in his mission will demonstrate to the enemies of Christ that they were mistaken in their judgment of Jesus. He will prove that Christ was the Son of God and was in no way worthy of the condemnation pronounced on him nor of the death on the cross which was imposed upon him by the world. The Spirit will through the ages prove to the world that its notions about Christ are completely wrong.

The Spirit will show the world wrong about uprightness by showing that this uprightness is not attained through the world's subjective norms. The Paraclete will prove that real uprightness before God is achieved only through faith in the risen Christ who is exalted to the right hand of the Father. The rightness and justice of Christ's cause is vindicated since he has returned to the Father and since his enemies cannot approach the Father nor receive the Spirit. The Spirit will also make manifest the condemnation and defeat of Satan, the prince of this world, who temporarily has seemed to triumph over Christ. It will be the task of the Spirit to explain to the world the meaning of Christ's death and the fact of the defeat of Satan that has occurred with Christ's death and resurrection.

The Spirit will also continue Christ's education of the disciples. Christ, during his ministry, communicated the basic message of salvation to his disciples but did not explain it in detail. The message was still incomplete, and, as this passage in John points out, it would be the mission of the Spirit to bring out the further and deeper implications of the revelation of Jesus. This is a continuing role of the Spirit in the life of the Church. The faith of the disciples was still too weak and imperfect to understand all the ramifications of the Christ-mystery.

As the disciples grew in faith, the Spirit would impart to them a deeper knowledge and understanding of the mysterious plan of the Father which had been hidden from all eternity but was now revealed in Christ. It is the Spirit who would slowly and carefully direct the disciples, and after them the Church, into a deeper understanding of the work and life of Christ, into a deeper appreciation of the kingdom and the place of the Christian in it. One aspect of the mission of the Spirit is therefore a revelatory, prophetic, and teaching role. The Spirit reveals Christ and Christ's meaning to the world and to the people of God; he proclaims the saving message and teaches its meaning. But this feature of the Spirit's role is still only a part of the total mission of the Spirit. There are many other aspects since the mission of the Spirit truly encompasses all of Christian living.

It is also the mission of the Spirit to make us conscious of our sonship and to orient us to our goal, which is the fulfillment of the designs of the Father. It is part of the role of the Spirit to convince us that we have been made heirs to the kingdom and have a duty to creation.

The whole creation is eagerly waiting for God to reveal his sons. It was not for any fault on the part of creation that it was made unable to attain its purpose, it was made so by God; but creation still retains the hope of being freed, like us, from its slavery to decadence, to enjoy the same freedom and glory as the children of God. From the beginning till now the entire creation, as we know, has been groaning in one great act of giving birth; and not only creation, but all of us who possess the first-fruits of the Spirit, we too groan inwardly as we wait for our bodies to be set free (Rom. 8:19-23).

The above passage from the eighth chapter of Romans has been a puzzle in the past, but it may perhaps be clearer to us now. It would seem that Paul is telling us that the Spirit directs us to the freeing of creation from decay, to the restoration of all things to the Father. The Spirit's role is evidently concerned with man's conquest of the universe which is the inheritance given to the Christian. But this is to be done in Christ by the sons of God, for the coming of whom creation is eagerly waiting.

The Spirit, then, would seem to be orienting the people of God to the fulfillment of the primal command of Genesis to subdue and conquer the universe. There should be a recognition on the part of the people of God that the future of the material universe is in God and that it is our inheritance and our task. From this passage in Romans we get a glimpse of the Spirit's relation to the full establishment of the kingdom of God which will finally include all creation.

For this purpose the Spirit is engaged in building the Church.

There is a variety of gifts but always the same Spirit; there are all sorts of service to be done, but always to the same Lord; working in all sorts of different ways in different people, it is the same God who is working in all of them. The particular way in which the Spirit is given to each person is for a good purpose. One may have the gift of preaching with wisdom given him by the Spirit; another may have the gift of preaching instruction given him by the same Spirit; and another the gift of faith given by the same Spirit; another again the gift of healing, through this one Spirit; one, the power of miracles; another, prophecy; another the gift of recognising spirits; another the gift of tongues and another the ability to interpret them. All these are the work of one and the same Spirit, who distributes different gifts to different people just as he chooses (1 Cor. 12:4-11).

It is in and through the Church that the mission of Christ is furthered and finally completed in the Spirit. The Spirit raises up at the proper time the people endowed and prepared for the work that is necessary in given circumstances for the advancement of the kingdom. It is the task of the Spirit to see that the Church has the people she needs to work out and to accomplish the plan of the Father for the people of God at any given time and in any given circumstances. The mission of the Spirit is concerned with the building and completion of the kingdom under the aspects of both the goal and the means to achieve the goal. The Spirit must also see to it that the members of the people of God are suited to the task of the development of the kingdom.

The Spirit is likewise necessary for the growth of the individual in Christ. This growth in holiness is necessary for the accomplishment of the Father's plan. It would certainly be valueless for men to gain complete mastery over all of creation if they did not live in harmony and with a common goal. It is the Spirit who is to provide the strength, power, and love needed to accomplish this harmony. "What the Spirit brings is very different: love, joy, peace, patience, kindness, goodness, trustfulness, gentleness and self-control" (Gal. 5:22).

The Spirit also leads us into a deeper prayer-union with the Father. "The Spirit too comes to help us in our weakness. For when we cannot choose words in order to pray properly, the Spirit himself expresses our plea in a way that could never be put into words, and God who knows everything in our hearts knows perfectly well what he means, and that the pleas of the saints expressed by the Spirit are according to the mind of God" (Rom. 8:26-28). Elsewhere Paul tells us that the Spirit gives us strength in time of trial and the courage to live our lives in faith and in hope.

It should be clear that the mission of the Spirit is a many-sided reality, embracing all the aspects of Christ's priesthood. It is the role of the Spirit in the Church to sanctify the people of God, to proclaim the fullness of the mystery of Christ, and to rule the people of God in love and, through this rule, to rule all of the universe. The task of the Spirit is the continuation of the priesthood of Christ as a witness to what has been accomplished in Christ and as a call to future accomplishment on the part of the people of God. This very brief survey of the New Testament gives us some idea of the scope of the work of the Spirit.

The Spirit can be expected to further reveal in the Church the full extent of his mission when we are mature enough to understand it and to accept it. The work of the Spirit is a growing reality, a constantly deeper penetration into the mystery of the Christ-event. It is a growing reality in which we share through the granting of the Spirit given us in the sacrament of confirmation. We share in Christ's growth in stature as the Lord of the universe, and by our sharing we help accomplish this growth.

THE PRIESTHOOD OF THE CONFIRMED

It has been said before that the second stage of the establishment of the Christian priesthood is the sacrament of confirmation. It was also suggested that it would be of value to consider this sacrament as a sharing in the temporal mission of the Holy Spirit. In the light of this sharing, what are the ramifications of this mode of approach to the priesthood?

In general, it can be said that the mission of the Spirit is to bear witness to the work already accomplished in Christ and to make clear to men all the implications of the Christ-mystery. It can likewise be said that the general mission imposed on the Christian by confirmation is this vital, dynamic witness to the salvation achieved in Christ and to the mystery of Christ's continuing growth as the Lord of all creation. This, it would seem to be, is what was meant by Christ's statement: "when the Holy Spirit comes upon you you will be my witnesses not only in Jerusalem but throughout Judaea and Samaria, and indeed to the ends of the earth" (Acts 1:8). The study of the scriptures gives us more specific details of this work of witnessing that is imparted to us in the reception of confirmation. We should examine what sharing in the mission of the Spirit means in our lives as Christians and how it affects our priestly vocation.

One task of the Spirit is to lead the Christian to a fuller understanding of the Christ-mystery and to his place in the still unfolding Christ-event. This has several orientations in the life of the Christian in the light of his relation to his own growth in Christ, to the growth of the Church, and to the revelation to the world of the saving work of Christ. The Christian must learn the meaning of his own life and the christic importance of every situation of his life. He must in the Spirit grow in faith so that he can more clearly read the meaning of the Christian life in his circumstances.

All of the experiences of his life are moments of confrontation with Christ, and the growth in Christ of each one of us is dependent on our understanding of these experiences. The gift of the Spirit which we receive in confirmation is meant to help us grow in understanding. We, on the level of our own life, must learn the meaning of Christ in the twentieth century. In our lives we must live out the Christ-event and slowly learn what Christianity must mean in the present milieu. Christianity is not merely a credo to which we must subscribe. It is not merely a set of commands we must follow. Christianity, without denying the existence of a body of beliefs or a group of commandments, is, above all, the personal meeting of Christ and the Christian in the many varied experiences of daily life.

It is one part of the Spirit's mission to lead us to an understanding of the Christ-mystery in our lives. If our priestly life, in virtue of confirmation, is a sharing in this mission of the Spirit, then it is part of our priesthood to reflect on our daily meetings with Christ. To the best of our ability and according to our talent and training we must live a conscious christic life. This is the only way in which we can come to a full appreciation of the meaning of our Christian lives. But we do not live in a vacuum either. We must articulate to the people of God the meaning that Christ has for us. The understanding of the Church about Christ and Christ's meaning for the twentieth century must grow, and this growth is predicated on the experience of all of God's people.

We must always remember that the Church is a reality that is both human and divine. In this she is like her Lord and she is like us. She is not wholly divine nor is she wholly human. She cannot divorce herself from her divine orientation nor can she remove herself from the material context in which she is embedded. She can never allow herself to remain aloof from the culture and to live out her Christ-life in some vacuum of her own choosing. She is forced by her very nature to live in the real world. To accomplish this task in a meaningful way she cannot rely completely on the thoughts of her theologians or on the life-experiences of the pastors of the flock.

These thoughts will never be sufficient for the true growth

of the Church, especially in the present situation in which the problems of the pastors bear little relation to the serious difficulties facing the majority of the people of God. There has been at work in the Church for the last several centuries a complex series of influences which has more or less effectively removed the theologians and the ordained priests from the cultural milieu and, consequently, from the everyday problems facing most Christians. Vatican II, however, has issued a stirring call to all Christians to live out their priesthood. We, all of us, pastors, theologians, and laity, must have the courage to answer this call with full faith in the guidance of the Spirit.

THE MISSION OF PROPHECY

We must proclaim to the other members of God's people that Christ is active in us and that the Spirit is guiding us. We must inform the Church of the problems we face in day-to-day Christian living, and we can never rest until she hears us. We must somehow get the Church to listen to our awareness of problems of a scope that is broader than our own personal lives, problems which concern the broader sweep of human culture and of the Church's place in that culture. Doctors, for example, must keep the Church informed on medical advances that have moral or dogmatic import. Lawyers and scientists must never hesitate to insist on a hearing when they become aware of problems that are developing.

Today there are a whole series of discoveries and a vast complexus of cultural forces that will confront the Church with problems of a magnitude greater than she has had to face in centuries. It is not difficult to run through a long list of them: war, hunger, poverty, sterilization, abortion, eugenics, the revolutionary discoveries in the life sciences and especially in genetics, the potential of mass media of communication, and so on and so on. Each Christian must do his best to acquaint the Church with problems of this nature of which he may be aware. This is a prime aspect of our sharing in the Spirit. We have to make ourselves heard, even should it seem that the leaders of the Church are unwilling or unable to listen.

This aspect of our priesthood will require tremendous patience, perseverance, courage, and, above all, charity. The general hesitance on the part of the leaders of the Church is very rarely a question of ill will. More often than not it is a question of not sharing the same vision of need or of hope for the future, and possibly of not sharing the same movement of the Spirit. We must remember that the Spirit does not act in the same way with each of us but assimilates himself and his activity to the talent, background, and social condition of each one of us.

When the Spirit urges us strongly and presents us with a vision and a dream, there is no guarantee that he will present it to others. In fact, we must reconcile ourselves to the realization that he probably will not. It becomes, in virtue of our priesthood, our task to bring this dream into reality in the Church. Each one of us has a role of importance to play in the realization of the entire vision of the Church. If the vision is truly from the Spirit, then there will come with it a deep sense of urgency together with the patience to accept delay and seeming indifference, with perseverance fed by a courageous faith in the ultimate acceptance of the dream, and with the charity and tolerance to live with human weakness, both our own and that of others.

Every Christian must accept this Spirit-role in the Church

and must realize that the Spirit is active in him and in others. Bishops, theologians, and ordained priests can never presume that they are the only recipients of the Spirit. They must listen in humble faith to all Christians and remember that it may very well be in this *listening* that the Spirit is most fully active in their lives. The faithful must speak and articulate to the Church their Christian experiences. Pastors must judge and weigh all they hear and under the impulse of the Spirit speak about these experiences. All must speak and all must listen.

No Christian has a monopoly on the Spirit nor does any Christian carry within himself the total vision that the Spirit is imparting to the people of God as a whole. There will, undoubtedly, be conflicts in this mutual interplay between the pastors and the people for the very reason that none of us can be the bearers of the full message of Christ and the complete inspiration of the Spirit. These difficulties in communication must be met with charity and with tolerance and with patience, all of which are hallmarks of the authentic presence of the Spirit. The hierarchy and the laity are in no sense enemies. We are all committed, or should be committed, to the same goal. All of us must be interested in the authentic growth of the Church and in her increasing effectiveness in building the kingdom of God. We must treat each other with mutual respect, understanding, and love. We must live in harmony and never permit enmity or what Paul calls "party-spirit."

In addition to our priestly articulation in the Church of the vision of Christianity which we have come to with the help of the Spirit, there is another very important aspect to this prophetic mission of the Spirit. Our priestly vocation of prophecy is to witness to the salvation that has already been won for man in Christ. We must move into the world and proclaim the saving message of Christ to all men. In confirmation we are given the power to be witnesses to Christ "in Jerusalem, Judaea and to the very ends of the earth."

We belong in the world and we must join with all men of good will in the search for the meaning of man, of man's progress, and of man's destiny. We must bring Christ to contemporary society and culture, but to do this we must understand the culture and Christ's relationship to that culture. We must move into scholarship, medicine, law, science, and all legitimate forms of human activity, and aid all of mankind in the search for a deeper understanding of the mystery of creation. Our proclamation to the world of Christ and Christ's saving presence cannot take the form of dogmatic statements. We cannot move into the cultural situation with a priori solutions to questions, all the ramifications of which we do not understand.

We have stressed many times that the Church is a growing, dynamic reality. The Body of Christ was not born fully grown in any respect. We must grow along with the growth of mankind in knowledge, in social patterns, and, truthfully, in every way. It is not merely a matter of policy or politics that we move into the world in a spirit of search or quest. We are pilgrims and we have not reached the end of our journey. We have a God-given task to perform and the God-given dynamism for growth in the performance of this mission.

We have all heard it said that the Church possesses all truth, and this is certainly true insofar as Christ is the Truth.

But the Church has not come to her full sharing in Christ. Until she does, she cannot be said to possess all truth. Indeed, it would seem that no small part of her mission is the integration of the truths that she has laboriously discovered with the truth that is Christ. The Church, and the individual Christian, cannot go into creation with the security of knowing all answers to all questions. As we have often said, it is her mission—her priestly mission—to search for answers and even to seek out the proper questions.

Our prophetic task as priests is the proclamation to the world of as full a revelation of Christ's saving love as we possess at the moment and the searching with all men for a deeper understanding of creation and man's place in it as a son of God. It is part of the prophetic role of the Christian priesthood to proclaim our dignity as sons of God and at the same time to search for a fuller understanding of just what it means to be a son of God. The prophetic aspect of the Christian priesthood is the proclamation of the wonderful saving work of God to ourselves, to the Church, and to the entire world. But this is not the totality of the Christian's sharing in the temporal mission of the Spirit. We must also consider this priestly sharing under the aspects of sanctification and ruling. We must be aware of our role of growing union with God—our union and that of the Church and of the entire sweep of creation.

THE MISSION OF SANCTIFICATION

We have spent much time on a consideration of the prophetic role of the Spirit, but we must not allow ourselves to consider this role merely as a collecting and discussing of ideas. If this were true, then we would be engaged in a mere intellectual exercise. We can never forget that the prophetic dialogue we have been discussing is but one element of the priestly mission in which we share. Paul tells us, "If I have the gift of prophecy, understanding all the mysteries there are, and knowing everything, and if I have faith in all its fulness, to move mountains, but without love, then I am nothing at all" (1 Cor. 13:2). Love for a Christian can mean only one thing—union with Christ. We have received, in the sharing in the mission of the Spirit in confirmation, the mandate to love, to penetrate creation with the self-gift of the Triune God. This love-impregnation is essential to the Christian task, and the success of the ruling aspect of Christ's priesthood is totally dependent on it. We shall treat this sanctifying role in itself and later we shall consider it again in its relation to the ruling mission.

The Spirit leads us into a deeper prayer-union with the Father. The Spirit pleads for God's people and expresses to the Father the yearnings that we cannot express. The Spirit is the bond of love that flashes from the Father to the Son and from the Son to the Father. It is the Spirit which also binds the Father in love to his sons and the sons to the Father. In the Spirit, we must come into a deeper and more conscious union with the Father.

In the Spirit, we must always become more conscious of our sharing in the nature of God and must more consciously integrate our humanity with the divinity in which we share through baptism. We must come to know Christ more intimately and love him more fully and through this knowledge and love gain insight into our union with the Father. This is the process of the Christian life which was only initiated with our baptismal sharing in the life and love and power of the Triune God. As in baptism we became partners in the Trinitarian love-life, in confirmation we are committed to a growing maturity in our sharing of this love-life. We are committed to a growing consciousness, in faith, of what it means to be a Christian, of what it means to be given the privilege to share God's love and to bring this love to other men and to all of creation.

The love of a Christian for Christ is a personal love. Each of us is growing into Christ, becoming more and more like Christ while never losing our own identity. It is not an accident that scripture speaks of this love-relation in terms of marriage. Married love is the closest love-union that we know and hence is apt to describe the growing love-life of the Christian and Christ. It is an integration of personalities, a growing into one, without each partner losing his own personal identity. In his relation to Christ the Christian should devote himself to Christ, he should come to think like Christ, anticipate his desires, and do whatever must be done to fulfill those desires.

In this growing together, Christ will give himself to the Christian more fully, will give of his life, his love, and his power. The Christian will become each day more like his Savior and become more a "Christ-among-men." He will live out his life according to the will of Christ as it is revealed to him in every situation of his life. He will develop a christic instinct and almost without reflection will apply Christ to the world in which he moves.

This last statement reveals a necessary orientation in this sanctifying process, the application of love to the world. The love-life of the Christian with Christ, as intimate and inexpressible as it is, is not meant to be exclusive. It is to be shared, to be spread to others. If not spread to others, it will wither and die and cease to have any meaning or life. Paul tells us in many places in his letters that the Law is summed up in love for the neighbor. "My brothers, you were called, as you know, to liberty; but be careful, or this liberty will provide an opening for self-indulgence. Serve one another, rather, in works of love, since the whole of the Law is summarised in a single command: *Love your neighbour as yourself*" (Gal. 5:13-14). As John tells us, "Anyone who says, 'I love God', and hates his brother, is a liar, since a man who does not love the brother that he can see cannot love God, whom he has never seen. So this is the commandment that he has given us, that anyone who loves God must also love his brother" (1 Jn. 4:20-21).

We must always remember that we share in the love of Christ, which is the love of God. This love is always creative and always productive. Because it is this love in which we share, our love should be productive of Christ in others. Through our union with Christ and through the presence of the Spirit within us, we grow more deeply into Christ and become in some mysterious way more and more Christlike. But as we read in scripture, this love-union must be shared with others.

As Christians, what we normally think of as human love is not without its divine element. Our love of nature is really a christifying love, a love which is productive of some type of divinizing effect. When we, as Christians, show appreciation, respect, and love for the beauty of creation and its place in the plan of the Father, we bring Christ to it and it to Christ. This is even more true of our treatment of our fellow-

men. By our attitudes, words, and action we can bring
Christ to others, we can deepen their love for Christ and
their union with the Triune God. We do this even through
what we are accustomed to consider as purely human love.
But for a Christian there is no such thing as merely human
love since we share in Christ. The expression of this love for
others depends on our own union with Christ.

To fulfill our priestly role of sanctifying, we must love first
of all our brothers and sisters in Christ—in the Church—
and, finally, love all men and creation. This love is not some
kind of general good will. It is a very concrete reality. It
begins in the family and then moves out into the neighborhood, into the business world, into local politics, and so on.
It demands that we give of our resources, our time, and even
our persons to those with whom we live and work. It means
concern for those whom we will never see but whom we
know are in need. It means concern for the poverty-stricken,
the ill, the lame, and the blind. It means sympathetic concern for those of our brothers who go to sleep hungry, who
do not have the means even to avert starvation, and who
must live in conditions that are far below those needed to
allow a life commensurate with human dignity.

Christian love requires a sympathetic openness to those
struggling with crises of conscience, with those who have
fallen for one reason or another from union with Christ. It
demands that we do what we can to ease the loneliness of
the bereaved, the trials of old age, the pain of sickness or of
mental anguish. It requires that we give of ourselves to those
in need. It means that we devote ourselves to the conquest of
all the evil in the world even though we may see no effect
from our efforts. Our sharing in Christ's love should not

allow us to throw up our hands in despair. We can affect that portion of creation with which we come into contact. We can, by giving of ourselves, of our time, our talent, our training, and our material resources, remake the world through the life, love, and power of Christ which we share. This is no small part of the task of the priesthood.

By becoming holier ourselves we also strengthen the Church. As members of the Body of Christ our holiness is inextricably bound to the strength of the whole Body. The holier the individual is, the holier the Church will be. The greater the union of the Christian with Christ, the deeper will be the union of the whole people of God with Christ and the closer the Church will be to Christ. The effectiveness of the Church is intimately bound to her relationship with Christ which is not a static relation but one that should always grow. If the Church is to accomplish the mission entrusted to her, she must depend on the christic life of all her members. As each Christian lives, so the Church lives. If we are in ever deepening union with Christ, the mission of the Church will prosper for the simple reason that Christ and Christ's power and love are more present to her. It is our Christ-life that is the determinant of the progress of the kingdom.

Although the whole burden of the Church's mission rests totally on no individual Christian, the measure of her achievement is in part determined by each Christian. The success of the Church is greater or lesser in proportion to our conscious christic integration. Thus, another feature of our Christian priesthood is the growth of the Church in terms of holiness. By cooperating with Christ's love-overtures, we grow in holiness and make the Church holier.

Through the life of the individual Christian and through the activity of the whole people of God all of creation is successively divinized. Thus, our priestly work of sanctification is carried on, and Christ's sanctifying work is applied to creation as it exists now.

THE MISSION OF RULING

But, as was mentioned earlier, the prophetic and sanctifying elements of the Christian priesthood are in many ways subordinated to the ruling aspect. Just as was true of Christ's priesthood, the Christian's priesthood looks essentially to the lordship of Christ. Our priesthood is directed to the submission of all of creation to Christ and ultimately to the Father. To accomplish this goal of our priesthood we must enter fully into the world and transform it in Christ. We must recognize the value of human progress in all its forms. We must realize that man's conquest of the universe is intimately connected with the final establishment of the kingdom of God. The conquest of all of creation for the Father includes the material progress of mankind and mankind's growing control of all of the universe. We must be aware that this conquest of nature and this penetration of nature's mysteries is an essential part of the ruling role of Christ's priesthood.

There is a growing feeling among many Christians that this is an indispensable part of the Church's mission. We are beginning to imagine a universe in which all of creation is subject to the mere force of man's will. Although the fulfillment of this dream may lie far in the future, the dream is becoming an intellectual and spiritual impulse to a growing segment of Christian thought. We should be working toward this end. The view that all of creation will be destroyed on "the last day" is yielding to the notion that creation has an eternal destiny in the life of God and will not be annihilated. Paul's statement of "freeing creation from its bondage to decay" is now being applied to the growth of man's domination over creation. Paul seems to be saying that in Christ we are to free creation.

Mankind is working toward the control of nature. It does not take a particularly shrewd observer to see that man's progress toward this goal is rapidly accelerating. Thinkers like Teilhard de Chardin see in the modern world the beginning of man's psychic development, and, if true, this holds out the promise of even greater progress for man. But it should seem clear that man's total control over nature is not sufficient for a goal. In his progress toward this goal of total mastery, man must also learn to master himself. If man reaches the stage of domination over creation by the mere force of his will, he must have a will that is in harmony with those of his fellowmen. The will of one man with such control would have to be such that it takes into account the convenience and need of other men and must also be in close relation with the common good of all men. Otherwise, the result of such mastery would be feuds, war, and ultimately the destruction of such a hard won mastery.

This is the kind of mastery we see in our own day, and future generations will see it with an even starker clarity. As man progresses and slowly unravels the mysterious skein of nature, his power to destroy increases proportionally. We stand in the shadow of atomic and nuclear holocaust, but we cannot even predict the threat of extinction that will lie over mankind one hundred years from now. We live outlined against the garish light of thermonuclear destruction. Yet, in the future man may have to face the possibility of the destruction of mankind through genetic selection. These fears are veiled from us, but history should give us enough evidence to show that technological progress, as magnificent as it certainly is, of itself will not be sufficient for the true progress of man.

We, as Christians, must enter into this tremendously exciting and productive surge of man. Those of us with the ability and training should be deeply engaged in the scientific and technological activity of man, recognizing it as of tremendous value and importance to the Church and to all men. We should know sleepless nights spent in pursuing an elusive idea and we should know the joy of discovery. We should live the monotonous day-after-day search for answers, with the creative thrust of the mind forging questions. We cannot be aliens to man's progress since this latter is unbreakably bound up with the kingdom of God. Those among us with creative ability in music or in poetry or in the plastic arts must enrich the human vision of reality with our works.

There is no one of us who has no talent or ability to offer to humanity in its progress. We must never allow ourselves to consider that our daily occupation is either divorced from Christianity or indifferent to the growth of the kingdom of God. There is no legitimate, nonsinful activity that does not reflect the Christ-life within us. We must put our talents, our dispositions, our occupations, and everything else that is ours at the service of man's progress. In doing so we penetrate man's progressive mastery of nature with the Christ-life that we share.

As Christians we must never hesitate to be in the forefront of the struggle for man's growth. This is where we belong. We owe to mankind the unstinting gift of all our abilities. But the gift, the absolutely necessary gift, that we bring to this pioneering growth of man is Christ. This gift offers the essential key to man's enjoyment of the mastery of creation. It was said that technological progress is not enough. Nor is a humanistic approach to reality sufficient for man's success in the task of the submission of nature to his will.

To accomplish the final and complete mastery of all of creation, man must master his own greed, envy, brutality, and passion. In a word, man must master himself and live in perfect harmony with all other men. Only in Christ, only in the love of Christ, is this complete and perfect socialization to take place. Only when all men have come to share the life and love of Christ will man's conquest of the universe be complete. We need merely to look at the daily newspapers to realize how far we are from this goal of complete human harmony.

If indeed man is building a new world, then all priests of Christ must be the cement holding it together. If man places brick upon brick in this structure, it must be Christians who bind them together. As man progresses and adds to his mastery over nature, we must apply the love of Christ to this progress. This is the ultimate task of our priesthood: to penetrate human progress with a love born of the love of Christ. This is our supreme sacerdotal mission: to serve mankind by giving Christ to men.

Only in the self-giving of Christ will man find the harmony needed to complete his progress and to set the capstone on the splendid work of his hands. This will be the advent of the sons of God for which creation is so eagerly longing.

Only when man ceases to seek himself in all things and only when he, in deep union with Christ, gives himself without stint and without selfishness—only then will man be able to say that, in Christ, he has built the new Jerusalem.

It is this goal—man's complete mastery over creation and his total mastery of himself in Christ—to which our priesthood is dedicated. It is to this end that we proclaim Christ's life, death, and resurrection, and it is to this end that we live Christ's life, death, and resurrection in our own lives. We must call men's attention to Christ and we must live his life to show them the limitless possibility of the future. We must make clear to them the "wonderful works of God" and we must bring these works to greater fulfillment in our own lives. Our priesthood in all its aspects is no more than our "Christhood." It is this that the world must see in us and it is this that the world must desire for itself. Then, together with all men, we can build a universe ready to receive Christ when he again returns to us. Then will be the beginning.

Our priesthood, born in baptism and brought to maturity in the sacrament of confirmation, is our Christ-life. It is expressed in the proclamation to ourselves, to the Church, and to all men that we have indeed been saved and called to an eternal destiny in the inner life of the Triune God. It is the sanctification of ourselves, of the Church, and of the universe, the sanctification that will end only in the most complete divinization possible for creatures. This priesthood, finally, has as its goal man's total mastery of all of creation, and especially of himself, in Christ.

Then our priesthood shall be fulfilled, and Christ will return to accept this oblation of love from our hands and in turn will return it to the Father from whom it came. This is the splendid offering of our priesthood: the world mastered by the glowing love of Christ through our union with him. In an incandescent moment that will last forever our priestly ministry will be completed, and all of creation, from the smallest to the greatest, shall live forever in the glory of the Triune God, creation now fully revealed to us who, in Christ, accomplished in self-gift this design of the Father of all.

7. Holy Orders

WE have, to this point, considered the Christian priesthood in the light of the sacraments of baptism and confirmation. We have structured this consideration on the idea that the Church, as the prolongation of Christ in time and space, shares in a finite and created way in all of the activities of the Triune God. We have considered baptism in terms of the mystery of the sharing in the inner life of the Trinity, in the eternal processions in God. We have also treated confirmation in terms of a sharing in the temporal mission of the Holy Spirit. In this latter treatment we adopted the notion that the mission of the Spirit, in general, is the witnessing to the fact that Christ has redeemed us and, now in glory, is still engaged in the work of restoring all of creation to the Father, thus carrying out the design of the Father that had been hidden from all eternity.

We must now come to a discussion of the third Church-building sacrament, holy orders. As was indicated previously we shall consider this sacrament in terms of a sharing in the temporal mission of the Son of God, a sharing in the continuing redeeming work of Christ.

Before we enter into this latter question we wish to treat the sacrament in somewhat more practical terms. It is the bishop who is the recipient of the fullness of the sacrament of orders. The bishop is the one who participates most fully in the Headship of Christ and in his continuing redeeming mission. The man we call the ordained priest is, then, a sharer in the priesthood of the bishop. He is, by his reception of the sacrament of orders, ordained to be an assistant to the bishop. This is made clear in the ordination rite where he is called "the helper of the bishop." It is also seen in the fact that the ordained priest is limited in the exercise of the priesthood insofar as he cannot ordain other priests or cannot confirm without an express mandate, given under quite restricted circumstances, from the bishop. What we say about the sacrament of orders, then, is primarily predicated of the bishop and only secondarily of those we customarily call priests. With this point made we may come to the consideration of the priesthood of the ordained.

We have said before that the priesthood of the Christian is oriented to himself, to the Church, and to all of creation. This cosmic orientation is of prime importance. The new people of God does not exist in a vacuum, it is not isolated in the desert as the first people of God was isolated at Mount Sinai. It is directed to the world, to those who have not yet heard of Christ or who have not accepted him. We should always have at the forefront of our vision the apostles in the streets of Jerusalem preaching the good news immediately after receiving the Pentecostal gift of the Spirit. The prime occupation of the confirmational priesthood is this witnessing to the world.

In this context of the world-directedness of the Christian priesthood in response to the Spirit's impulse, we must consider the special aspect of the ordained priesthood. Without any diminution in the opportunities and obligations of the priesthood arising from baptism and confirmation, the priesthood of the ordained is oriented in a special way to the needs of the people of God. Its purpose is to provide means of sanctification to the faithful through the sacraments and the sacrifice of the Mass, to give the people of God a guide in matters relating to the message of Christ, and to rule the Church in service. The ordained priesthood, then, is established for the service of the faithful.

It is not easy, in the present state of theology on the priesthood, to make clear just what this sacrament really adds to the Christian priesthood in any area of life outside of liturgical practice and jurisdiction. The reason for this is found in the context of history. We are the heirs to an ordained priesthood that de facto has mostly confined itself to its liturgical and jurisdictional aspects. When we think of the priesthood, we immediately think of the parish priest. This is the model, developed over the centuries, on which we base our theology. Our whole thinking about the ordained priesthood, it would seem, has been centered around a historical accident. The diocese, or the parish, is a geographical unity that has, since the very early days of Christianity, served as the basis of Christian life. Our idea of the ordained priesthood has been very largely constructed on the basis of the diocese and the parish. The bishop is the local bishop, and the priest is the man who is connected with the parish church.

There has also been a heavy juridical stress in the past on the priesthood. The priest has been considered as placed in charge of the people of God. There can be no doubt that this is true in many senses, but there may be some question of whether it is true in the way that this authority has been actually used in some parts of the western Church. There seems to have been an overemphasis on the canonical and the jurisdictional aspects of the priesthood.

The priest is ordained to sanctify, to instruct, and to rule the people of God. Unfortunately, at certain times and in some places this fact has relegated the laity to a position of inferiority in a Church in which there can be no class of elite, in which we all form one elite, even though there exist different offices and functions in the Church. The priest had all the answers and made all the decisions, sometimes dominating the consciences of the faithful and acting more as a tyrant than as the servant of the servants of God. The question at issue, really, is whether the notion of the ordained priesthood that most of us either consciously or subconsciously maintain is an adequate expression of that priesthood. It would seem that it is not.

First of all, is the ordained priesthood adequately expressed by the liturgical and jurisdictional aspects of the life of the Church over which the ordained priest presides? If it is, it is difficult to see why the Church has always encouraged at least some of her ordained priests to pursue lives of scholarship, lives that involve for them a severe limitation in liturgical participation. In fact, the Church has never clearly given a satisfactory theoretical reason, based on a theology of the sacrament of orders, why priests should engage in, for instance, the natural sciences. Yet, her instinct has told her that it is important that there be men consecrated by orders engaged in the pursuit of knowledge on all fronts. At one time it could have been argued that she did this merely because the laity was too poorly educated to engage in scholarship. But this is not the case now, at least in the United States and in Europe.

Yet, Vatican II exhorts some priests to devote their lives to scholarship and not only in the so-called sacred sciences. Is this a legitimate pursuit for the ordained? How does it fit in with their call to sanctify, to proclaim, and to rule? Could it be that such work is a very important element of the total call of the ordained priesthood? While it is not wise to build a theology on a special case, it is equally unwise and unprofitable to have a theology that does not account for such cases. We hope, in the following pages, to take at least a faltering step toward a broader notion of the ordained priesthood. The presumption underlying this different approach is that, by the sacrament of orders, the ordained Christian participates in the continuing total redeeming work of Christ.

PARTICIPATION IN THE HEADSHIP OF CHRIST

The ordained priesthood shares in the Headship of Christ. Vatican II tells us, "Therefore, while it indeed presupposes the sacraments of Christian initiation, the sacerdotal office of priests is conferred by that special sacrament through which priests, by the anointing of the Holy Spirit, are marked with a special character and are so configured to Christ the Priest that they can act in the person of Christ the Head" (Decree on the Ministry and Life of Priests, Chapter I, Number 2). In view of this participation in Headship it should seem clear that it is the primary task of the ordained priesthood to strengthen and deepen the life of the Body of Christ.

The sacerdotal office in the Church looks then to the making of the priesthood of the laity a more effective instrument in its triple role of sanctification, prophecy, and rule. The ordained are to serve all of the members of the Church so that all these members, the ordained included, share as deeply as possible in the Christ-mystery and carry to full completion the continuing mission of Christ to restore all things to the Father. To carry out this service to the people of God the ordained priesthood should be active in explicitly aiding the sons of God in carrying out every aspect of their priesthood.

Two phases of the work of the ordained, dispensing the sacraments and preaching, are well-known to us. The sacramental life of the Christian, though it looks also to the ruling aspect of the Christian priesthood, seems primarily directed to the union of the Christian with Christ and the union of Christians among themselves. The work of preaching and of proclamation is basically directed to a deeper understanding of the life and goal of the individual and, ultimately, of the Church. These are familiar to us. But the relationship of the ordained to the nonordained, insofar as the ruling aspect is concerned, has not been too precisely delineated. This ruling relationship has been treated in a much too legalistic fashion in the past and, it would seem, in a totally inadequate fashion.

At this point it might be of value to consider what we have called the continuing total redeeming role of Christ. Then we shall be in a better position to discuss the participation of the ordained in this redeeming activity. We do not mean that Christ's redemptive life, death, resurrection, and ascension were inadequate. We do not mean that he did not redeem all or that he did not redeem fully. What we do mean is that he did not redeem automatically. Man must respond positively to Christ's redemptive mission. God is calling us as human beings, as free agents. Man must respond freely to the divine initiative. In a sense, then, all men have been saved since all men can now approach the Father in Christ. All men have not been saved in the sense that all men must of necessity approach the Father in Christ in each situation of everyday life. It is still possible to escape the redeeming love-clasp of the divine hands.

Man can, in virtue of his free will, reject God and God's offer of himself to man. This rejection must be recognized as not only an individual refusal to accept God, but also as a cosmic denial, to some extent, of divine love and divine life. If it is true that, in our positive response to God's overtures, we can affect all of creation and aid in subjecting it to the Father's love, it must be true that a negative response to God on the part of an individual hinders and weakens the return of creation to the Father. The individual can not only cut himself off from God but also he can influence others to reject God and can lead at least a small part of creation away from God. This is clearly within the capacity of an individual, and it is likewise clearly within the capacity of families, communities, nations, and cultures.

We have, in the twentieth century, seen sufficient evidence of godless ideologies, national policies, and cultural influences. We have looked on very sophisticated and efficient efforts at genocide, mass murder, and even propaganda aimed at destroying the moral consciousness of large segments of mankind. The technological progress that can be utilized to the growth and strengthening of the kingdom of God can also be applied to the weakening of this kingdom.

What can be applied to man's glorious growth as a son of
God can also, and possibly even more efficiently, be used to
reduce man to slavery to himself and his appetites. Technological competence can be used as a vehicle for building,
in Christ, the perfect society or it can be used to negate the
dignity of man. It can be used to apply more adequately to
men the redemption won for us by Christ, or it can to a
greater or lesser extent stifle the activity of the Spirit. All
this is a result of God loving us so much as to give us freedom. It is the outgrowth of the desire of the Father to raise
up sons rather than mere subjects.

It is clear to anyone who has taken the time to investigate
that man has not reached the goal of divine life. It must be
evident that Christ's redemptive work has not been completed, neither in the lives of communities nor in those of
individuals, neither in the lives of non-Christians nor in
those of Christians. We are all aware of the need in our own
lives for a continuing work of redemption, for growth in the
sonship we have received in baptism. We are clearly aware
of our weakness, our ignorance, and our lack of love. It is to
these individual needs that the work of continuing redemption looks.

But it is not solely to these that this redemptive activity is
to be applied. It must be an influence in the culture and
activity of the community, of the nation and, ultimately, of
all mankind. If the culture is not made christic, then the
mission of redemption is radically incomplete and tragically
unfulfilled. It is to this that the ordained priesthood looks—
to the strengthening and growth of the Body of Christ, to
the growth of Christ in the individual members of this Body
and in the totality of the cosmos.

The sacraments themselves are a sign of this continuing

total redeeming action that is being carried on in the Church. The sacraments are vehicles for constituting the Church, for prolonging the presence and mission of Christ in the world. They are also means for a restoration of union with Christ if it has been lost or for the deepening of this personal love-relation which has been established in baptism. They are signs of Christ's redeeming presence, and they effect that presence in the one who receives them and in the Church and in all of creation through the life and activity of the recipient. In the past, however, we have considered the sacramental life to be almost the total expression of this continuing redemptive activity of the ordained priesthood. There has been mention of preaching but only as a thing of rather minor importance, though this attitude is now changing.

Perhaps now, in the light of the decrees of Vatican II, we can catch a glimpse of a broader arena of activity for the ordained priesthood. The priesthood, first that of the bishops and, then, with them that of their helpers, must look beyond the individual "care of souls." We must realize that the fulfillment of the continuing redeeming mission of Christ must be of as great a scope as Christ's mission itself. The ordained priesthood must engage itself in sanctifying, witnessing to, and ruling all of creation. It must dedicate itself to the total redemptive mission of Christ, which is to return all things to the Father. It must exercise its shared Headship in Christ in every authentic aspect of life. The power of Christ must be brought to bear on individuals and on cultures, on men and on all material creation. The ruling aspect of the priesthood of orders must embrace the entire scope of created reality.

We said before that the office of the ordained priesthood looks primarily to the sanctification, education, and ruling of the people of God. But this role cannot be separated from the cosmic scope discussed above since the mission of the people of God is directed to all of creation. The redemptive Headship of Christ in which the ordained Christian shares must permeate the Body of Christ at every level of its life. It must be available to the Body in every one of the manifold ways in which the Christian confronts reality.

This continuing of the mission of Christ is expressed in sacrament and sacrifice and in explaining the saving word of Christ. It is articulated in the proclamation that, though we are already saved, we are still being saved. It is the role of the ordained priesthood to aid all of the people of God in their growing mastery over the universe and in their concomitant deepening union with Christ. Those whose office in the Church is to sanctify, prophesy, and rule the people of God must bring the consecrated saving activity of Christ to all the faithful in every area of human life.

It was stated before that we really have no positive evidence to regard the parochial priesthood as a totally adequate expression of the priesthood of orders. It is true that this expression of the sacerdotal office has had a long and glorious tradition. It is equally true that it has been successful in building and strengthening the kingdom of God. But we must never allow ourselves to consider the success of such an expression the sole determining factor in our consideration. It must be pointed out again that to say the parochial and diocesan priesthood is not an adequate expression of the totality of the priesthood is not to say that it is a poor expression of the priesthood or one that has outlived its usefulness. But there may be other equally important expressions of the reality that is the ordained priesthood.

In our own times we are becoming aware of the positive

human value that is inherent in human progress and in the growth of human cultures. We are also becoming more aware of the inadequacy of the parish and diocesan structure to fully meet the need of penetrating these cultures and bringing the love and power of Christ to bear on them. In this country, historically, the center of Christian life has been the parish, and the parish priest has been the dominant model from which our theology of the ordained priesthood has been drawn. We are not too familiar with those priests whose primary mission is not liturgical or cultic, even though there are many such priests among us. To say that this segment of the clergy is not fully exercising its priestly life would be a very harsh statement.

Before we can consider adding new forms of expression of the ordained priesthood, it is essential that we should develop a broader notion of the nature of the Christian priesthood. This we are attempting to do in describing the priesthood in terms of the sharing in Christ's continuing work of redemption, in terms of the consecrated priest's participation in the Headship of Christ.

In the last few decades there has been a growing idea in the Church that the technological control of the universe by man is very intimately linked with the growth of the kingdom of God, that it is not just something of temporary usefulness that will end in ashes on the last day. Though Vatican II rightly stated that human progress in itself is not to be identified with the kingdom of God, yet it would seem that human progress christified by the people of God is to be identified with the new Jerusalem. If this is not the structure (to use Paul's image) that we are building, then what are we actually doing?

Are we passing through the world, affecting it, and then departing from it, all the while considering it merely the stage on which the human drama is played out? Do we consider the created universe as merely a stage prop that will be destroyed when the last curtain is brought down? Or is it, indeed, something that will, when true human progress has reached its ultimate expression, be brought through man's agency into the all-embracing arms of the Triune God? If this latter is true, then the Headship of Christ must be brought to bear on every authentic aspect of creation. It should be clear that if Christ's Body is to ultimately include all of the universe, then this can be achieved only when Christ's Headship over all has been established, "so that he should be first in every way" (Col. 1:18). This "every way" must include the whole of reality that has been reclaimed from the power of sin through our living out of the Christian priesthood.

This ruling aspect must be effected through the sanctification of the individual and the proclamation to all the universe of Christ's saving message. It must also be brought about by the priestly concern on the part of both the ordained and nonordained Christian for the christification of human culture in all its various aspects. We must not focus all of our priestly attention on the care of individuals. Some of our priests, again both ordained and nonordained, must devote their lives more or less exclusively to cultural pursuits. If our notion of the mission of the Christian priesthood, in all its modes of expression, is focused on the lordship of Christ, then we should not make the mistake of thinking that anything divorced from the strictly cultic is a nonpriestly activity.

The christification of the culture should be an effort of the total Church, Head and members. It should be a partnership of priests, an effort shared by the members of the people of God and by those who participate in the Headship of Christ. The ordained must not be present merely in the role of overseers and directors of such an apostolate. They should be there as bearers of the continuing redemptive presence of Christ. Those of the nonordained who are highly trained should be active not merely as glorified messenger boys but as the bearers of the Spirit. In this way, through the presence of those whose priesthood is the sharing in the mission of the Spirit, actively joined by those sharing in the continuing mission of the Son, the whole of the divine activity toward creation will be brought to bear in a created way on the growth of mankind.

With man's control over the universe growing at an accelerating rate it is imperative that the Church move much more decisively to engage some of her priests in a culturally oriented apostolate. That this is to be predominantly the work of nonordained priests should be clear. But it seems equally necessary that they should be joined by some of the ordained. This apostolate ideally should be one in which the nonordained are most needed, but it should not be exclusively conducted by them. This is not because they are poorly trained or not to be trusted or somehow inferior. It is because the whole Church, Head and members, should undertake this vital work. If, indeed, the mission of Christ is incomplete without the mission of the Spirit and if the mission of the Spirit has no meaning apart from that of Christ, it should be evident that the participated missions of Christ and the Spirit are both needed for the successful carrying out of the mission of the Church.

The function of the ordained priesthood, it seems, should not be limited to the cultic. Its scope should not be limited to those aspects of the Christian priesthood over which the nonordained have no power simply because they are not given that power. This would be a very negative norm on which to judge the scope of the ordained priesthood. If the ordained priest is limited to the sacristy, so to speak, it is the mission of the whole Church which would be made poorer. If the function of the priesthood of orders, including both the episcopate and the presbyterate, is to serve the people of God, it must serve the people of God fully in every phase of their work to restore all of creation to the Father. If the people of God, through their Christ-life, are to sanctify and reduce to Christ's will all the facets of creation that have authentic value, then the ordained priesthood must serve them in every stage of this process.

Some of the ordained should be appointed to serve them in their professional lives just as others are to be designated to serve them in the more personal aspects of their lives. It would seem fitting that the shared Headship of Christ be made active in the professional sphere where much of the apostolate of the nonordained is pursued. It does not appear to be reasonable to limit the continuing redeeming activity of Christ to the personal lives of the people of God. Even if this is the way we have always proceeded, does this mean that the ordained priesthood is by its nature so circumscribed? We need only to look at the way Christ lived his priesthood to see that the consecrated priesthood should also be concerned directly in the professional activity of the people of God. Remember that Christ spent a large segment of his priestly life as a carpenter. It does not seem that we should casually write this off. It should, at least, make us pause to reexamine our notions of the function of the ordained priesthood.

We are not saying that every ordained priest should engage in an apostolate that is directly concerned with the problems and opportunities offered by human culture and technological progress. We are suggesting only that some, whose talents and interests are so oriented, should bring the redeeming power of Christ, that is theirs in virtue of the sacrament of orders, to bear on the work of the subjection of the universe to Christ through their direct cooperation with cultural growth and human progress. This is obviously a work to which all are not equally suited by ability and temperament.

An apostolate of this sort should be encouraged for those who are able to carry it on and are interested in it. It is not, and must not, be entered into solely in the spirit of "showing the flag." It would severely limit the effectiveness of such an apostolate to limit it to a solely apologetic aspect. It is not a question of engaging in this type of work merely to attempt to show people that we are aware of the existence of their culture or their particular subculture. This form of apostolate must be undertaken because in itself it is vital to the progress of mankind and of essential importance to the Church's growth in understanding revelation and the nature of her mission in its fullest scope.

What we have been saying can be summarized rather briefly. The priestly mission of the sons of God extends to every authentic aspect of creation. It is to be exercised in every legitimate occupation and under all circumstances of time, place, and culture. Their very Christian life, expressed in all its manifold opportunities and situations, is their priesthood. By their individual ability, training, and opportunities, both personal and occupational, the Spirit directs them and their efforts to the growth of the kingdom of God, and, ultimately, to the glorious fulfillment of the mission begun and still carried on by Christ: the restoration of all of creation to the Father. Their priesthood, the priesthood of the people of God, is directed to, and will at length achieve, the goal of the Father that all of creation come to share in the divine life and love of the Triune God.

The priesthood of the ordained, since it is a sharing in the Headship of Christ, is directed to strengthening the Body of Christ on every level of its life and activity. This service is to be expressed in aiding in the personal growth of each Christian priest into Christ. This aspect of the mission of the ordained priesthood is quite familiar to us all. It is carried out in the sacrifice of the Mass and the sacraments. It is also manifested in the preaching of the saving words of Christ. It is, in general, fostered in the life of the parish and of the diocese and can find at least an adequate fulfillment in this context.

But the priesthood of the faithful is also to be carried out in the professional activity of every Christian, in their cultural work, and in their efforts at aiding man in his increasing domination of the universe. Since this is a truly authentic and essential aspect of the Christian priesthood, every effort must be made to strengthen this type of apostolate and to bring to bear on it the productivity of Christ's redeeming activity. This is also to be part of the service that the ordained priesthood owes to the people of God. For a fuller expression of the totality of the ordained priesthood, to be found on the level of both the episcopate and the presbyterate, it would seem necessary to consider new forms of activity to supplement the work of the parish and of the diocese. Some aspects of this statement will be treated later.

What we have said is that the priesthood of orders in the Church has a mission of service oriented to the strengthening and deepening of the priesthood of the people of God. This service is needed at every level of activity of the Christian priesthood. Of its nature, then, the ordained priesthood is to be restricted only by the limits of the cosmic mission of Christ. The ordained priest is the servant of the nonordained in every aspect of Christian life and must bring to this activity in all its facets the continuing redeeming power of Christ.

8. Tentative Conclusions

WE have been treating of the Christian priesthood in a rather theoretical fashion. It has been stated that every Christian shares in the priesthood of Christ. We have developed the idea that every Christian is at every moment of his Christian life a Christ-bearer, a sanctifier, a prophet, and a ruler. We have considered the effects of baptism, confirmation, and orders in the process of building the totality of the Christian priesthood. A synthetic approach, such as the one used thus far, should result in a new view of the reality to which it has been applied. This is the burden of this chapter.

If we develop such a theory of the Christian priesthood, what ramifications must we consider? In what way will the functions of the priesthood be modified? What must be expected in terms of the daily life of the Christian and in the makeup of the Church? These questions bear essentially on the value of the approach used and the validity of the synthetic structure that has been developed. In other words, this theory that has been built must stand or fall on the practical conclusions that follow from it. What exactly are some of these ramifications? What would such a priesthood be like?

We have taken the priesthood of Christ as the basis of our

approach, a priesthood whose essential goal is the lordship of Christ. The accomplishment of this domination of all of creation through service in love is therefore the prime occupation of the Christian priesthood. This is a task equally shared by all Christians. In the manner in which we usually consider the priestly life of the Christian, it seems as if the layman is a very attenuated ordained priest and the man we call a priest is a watered-down version of a bishop. If we consider baptism as the sacrament of introduction into the priestly office, we get a much broader view of the priestly mission of every Christian. It seems that the general sacerdotal sacrament is baptism and that confirmation and orders are further specifications of our priestly involvement. It is hoped that such an approach will have an effect in promoting the dignity of the Christian priesthood.

A few centuries ago it was seriously proposed that the priesthood of the laity would find its full expression in the chanting of psalms in heaven. There seems to be a great misconception at work in considering the priesthood of the nonordained Christian as modeled on the priesthood of the ordained. It appears to be more reasonable to consider that the priesthood of the Christian is the fundamental concept and that the ordained priesthood carries a specific function within the Christian community of priests.

THE PRIESTLY STATE

From our theoretical development of a theology of the priesthood it should be clear that every Christian is, in virtue of his very Christ-union, a priest. By his dying and rising in Christ through baptism, he becomes involved in the triple function of sanctification, prophecy, and kingship. This is his through his sharing in Christ's life, love, and mission. All the elements of Christ's priestly mission are found in the priesthood of the Christian in a shared and created way.

The mission of the Christ-sharer is the domination of all of creation and the restoration of the universe to the Father. To accomplish this mission the Christian must grow into a deeper and more consciously integrated union with Christ. This is the sanctifying aspect of his priesthood. He must, in order to deepen this union, share Christ's love with other men—his fellow Christians first, and ultimately with all of mankind. He must accomplish this by living a life impregnated with the notion of service for others and by proclaiming to all men, by word and deed, the fact that we and all creation have been redeemed. By his growth in Christ and by his proclamation of Christ the Christian carries out the mission of Christ. This is the primal mission of the Christian priesthood, and this mission is not to be considered merely in terms of the ordained priesthood.

By the very fact that baptism introduces men into the priestly people of God, it should be clear that the baptismal priesthood is the foundation of all the priestly functions in the Church. Without this priesthood there can be no priesthood of orders. The ordained priesthood can exist only in the context of the baptismal "ordination" of the people of God and can, therefore, be understood only in this context. The ordained priesthood is established to serve the nonordained priests. The priesthood of the baptized does not grow out of the priesthood of the ordained. It is rather the other way around. An understanding of this should undoubtedly cause a revision in our manner of considering the priesthood.

We have stated on several occasions that baptism incorporates a man into the people of God, makes him a sharer in the life of the Triune God, and dedicates him and all his resources to the one mission that Christ gave the Church: the building and strengthening of the kingdom of God. By the very fact of his incorporation into Christ the Christian becomes irrevocably involved in the cosmic growth of Christ. His priesthood is this involvement in the sanctification of himself, the Church, and the universe; in the proclamation of Christ's saving death and resurrection; and in the establishment of the rule of Christ over all things. This cosmic mission is not confined to the ordained but is, rather, the privilege of all Christians. We have all been chosen by God as partners in the work of making all things new in Christ.

In baptism we are all called to live and grow in Christ and to exercise the power of Christ that is ours in virtue of our love-relationship with him. Within the context of this baptismal consecration there is no occasion in our lives in which we are not called to be the point of insertion between time and eternity, between God and creation. It is God's decree that has determined that the salvation won by Christ must be applied to all of creation by those creatures who have been united to Christ and who strive to grow into a conscious awareness of that union and the duties which grow from it. There is no situation in our lives when this union with the Father through Christ and in the Spirit is inoperative or unproductive. This we know only through faith, but it does appear reasonable.

We must not allow our christic power to be diminished by thinking that we are in union with God only when we are praying formally. Paul tells us that Christ is our vital principle now that we have been joined to him through baptism. This vital principle is not an on-again off-again reality for those earnestly striving to live out their Christian lives according to the will of God. It is functioning at every moment of every day. This union with the Father through Christ and in the Spirit is the Christian priesthood. Every act we perform under the seal of this union is a priestly act, an act of mediation between God and creation.

What we are saying here can be summarized quite briefly. Baptism is the sacrament which effects the priestly state. To be baptized means to be a priest. The sacraments of confirmation and orders add nothing essential to the priestly state beyond its further specification. In confirmation we are given the Spirit to guide our priestly activity and to give us the further strength needed to succeed in the carrying out of the Spirit's mission. In orders the Christian is given the function of sanctifying, teaching, and serving the people of God in a life of special sacramental dedication. Thus, the sacraments of confirmation and orders look to function rather than to the establishment of the priestly state of life. In them we receive a sacramental mandate and a sacramental strengthening to carry out the duties arising from the sharing in the missions of the Son and the Spirit.

It is our union with and our partnership in the love-life of the Triune God from which our priesthood arises. It is this Triune sharing that makes us sons of God and gives us a share in the mediatorial role that belongs preeminently to the Son of God. By becoming sons we become mediators, we are made priests. We are priests precisely in virtue of our trinitarian life and destiny. This is what it means to be sons of God.

In virtue of his incarnation, Christ was given the dignity of the high priesthood of the new law. It was not a dignity that he assumed on his own but one that was given him by the Father. So it is, too, in the functional priesthood which arises from the sacrament of orders. No Christian assumes this mission of continuing Christ's redeeming work but must be called to it by Christ. In being consecrated by orders he shares in the functions of Christ's priesthood. The reception of holy orders constitutes a new dedication, a new answer to the call of Christ. It does not seem to constitute a new state of life, but rather gives a special role and special powers to be used for the growth of the people of God.

This situation seems true of the mission of the Spirit also. The Spirit was sent to the Church to give her the strength and guidance she needs to foster the growth of the kingdom of God established by the life, death, and resurrection of Christ. This Pentecostal outpouring of the Spirit is repeated in the life of each Christian at confirmation. This reception of the Spirit gives to each recipient the mandate to proclaim to that part of creation with which he comes into contact that Christ has redeemed the world and that mankind has entered into the last age of history. He is directed to fulfill in his own life, in the Church, and ultimately throughout the universe the prophecy of Joel: "After this I will pour out my spirit on all mankind. Your sons and daughters shall prophesy, your old men shall dream dreams, and your young men see visions" (Joel 3:1).

The Christian must, by his Christlikeness in action and in words, make clear to the world that man's destiny lies with God. He must, in the Spirit and with the Spirit's power, aid all men in their effort to penetrate the mysteries of nature and then to dominate nature. The Christian must also bring to men, under the aegis of the Spirit, the harmony of will that can come only from man's sharing in Christ's love. The function of the confirmational priesthood is, in reality, the dedication of the total life of the Christian, personal and professional, to the building up of the kingdom of God. It is the Spirit-directed application of the priestly powers received by the Christian in baptism.

THE PRIESTLY FUNCTION

This means that the true Christian priesthood is granted to all in baptism. The double mission of the Son and the Spirit is then shared in a further specification of this priestly state. The nonordained are truly priests and bear the priestly dignity of sons of God. They are not at all to be considered as inferior in their priestly state to the ordained. The ordained and nonordained share the same priestly state; their functions, however, are different.

Paul tells us that there is one mission and many ministries. The one mission, shared by all the sons of God, is the priestly mission of the restoration of all things to the Father. The ministries are the means of accomplishing the mission. These differ for those who share in the Headship of Christ and for those who do not have a sacramental sharing in this office. The priestly functions of each Christian also differ in virtue of the talents, training, and opportunities of each. This should be true of both the ordained and the nonordained.

The priesthood of the faithful is to be expressed in the

love to be found in the home—the conjugal love of man and wife and the love and respect between parents and children. It is found in the communication of parents with their children and children with their parents. It is stated in the mutual concern of every member of a family for the other members and in the effort made daily by each to foster harmony in the home. It is expressed in the mutual discussion of problems and the united attempt to solve these problems. It is expressed in the care of a mother for a sick child and in the care of the father for the financial security of his family.

Anything, in short, that promotes harmony and cooperation, respect and love in the family is an exercise of the priestly role given to all Christians in baptism. All these things are a manifestation of the priesthood and a proclamation of the wonderful work that God has achieved. The Christian family, united in harmonious love, is a prophetic uttering of the presence of the Holy Spirit in the world.

The professional aspect of the Christian life is also a manifestation of the priesthood. This brings with it the privilege and obligation of bringing the Christ who dwells within us into the milieu in which we work. It means also bringing our work into the Church. The Christ in whom we share is deeply needed in our contemporary culture. This need cuts to the very heart of man struggling to perfect himself, the immediate society in which he lives, and the association of all men. Only in Christ are men ever to find the harmony needed to bring them to the full expression of their humanity.

Christ should be the contribution of the Christian to the society in which he lives and grows and attains as fully as possible the complete expression of himself. By doing his work as thoughtfully and as well as he can, each Christian contributes, according to his talent, training, and position, to the progress of the human race and to the more complete building up of the kingdom of God. The work of a Christian, whether it be intellectual or artistic, skilled or unskilled, manual or whatever, is not something that the Christian does in between periods of prayer. It is not something that is a necessary evil, merely a means of providing the necessities or even the luxuries for daily life. There can be absolutely no doubt of the importance of the latter, but a true, positive Christian vision of reality shows the occupation of the Christian in its full cosmic scope. The carrying out of a Christian's work is no small part of the manifestation of his priesthood.

There can be no doubt that this aspect of the Christian's life has been neglected. How many of us have heard sermons extolling human toil as merely a fitting sacrifice to be offered up because it is difficult. How often is the attitude expressed that it is truly unfortunate that we have to engage ourselves in labor, but it is the Christian's duty to make the best of what can only be called a bad situation? Can we possibly imagine Christ working at Nazareth with such an attitude? No matter what work we do, no matter how prestigious or how humble it is, we are serving others. We are serving our families, our neighbors, and, ultimately, all mankind.

Every human effort is needed in man's thrust toward progress on every level. The hierarchy's attitude over the last few centuries has not adequately encouraged Christians to foster this positive approach to their professional lives. Not that they actively discouraged such an approach. It is rather that they did not actively express their concern for progress on the human level. This, of course, must change.

The beginnings of a new positive theology of terrestrial values are discernible in the Constitutions and Decrees of Vatican II. The professional expression of the Christian priesthood is one that calls for extensive change in the life of the Church.

THE PRIESTHOOD IN THE PROFESSIONAL LIFE OF THE CHRISTIAN

It had been mentioned earlier that the unifying factor of the parish or diocese is one of geography. This is not a bad thing, but it is not as conducive to the Christian's occupational dedication to the priesthood as it is to other, more personal, aspects of the priesthood. Why are we not doing more to foster an official grouping of Christian's along professional lines? This is not a completely new concept in western civilization, as the medieval guilds testify. There have also been unofficial, or even quasi-official, attempts to foster a deeper christianizing of the professional aspects of our lives. But there has been no official attempt on a diocesan or supradiocesan, such as the national, level to utilize the tremendous apostolic potentiality available to the Church in the professions and in the arts.

A new structure, built alongside the parish and diocesan structure, could be of great value to the Church. It would not only enable her to penetrate modern culture in a more apostolically effective way but it would also be of help for her to understand that culture more deeply and more sympathetically. She could be more deeply cognizant of the trends of society and she could lead more effectively in the development of modern culture. How often have we seen the spectacle of the Church merely reacting to the culture and never helping to form the culture? How often have we seen her not only react, but react negatively to cultural processes, only in the end to back down? How destructive is this approach to the faith of the people of God? Is it God's will that we spend our lives merely reacting? Or is it God's will that we at least attempt to direct, in service to men, the cultural and technological growth of man and of society? If it is the latter, we had best make up our minds soon to make a serious effort to penetrate, understand, and give ourselves to man's growth. The time is short and the stakes are daily getting higher.

There are several revolutions of critical dimensions taking place in the world today. About some of these revolutions the Church is aware and is taking some action. She is aware of the political upheavals throughout the world, and as a body she is striving to at least set up some apparatus for peaceful settlements of conflicts. She is aware of the unrest in the world that springs from the tension between the have-not nations and the wealthy, highly technological nations. In the course of one generation, in the last thirty or forty years, the undeveloped nations have come to a realization of how short they fall of the wealth of the more developed nations.

People, it seems, can live in misery, squalor, and near starvation so long as they think that this is the common lot of most men. Once they learn that large segments of mankind have material prosperity that they never dreamed of, they become restless and restive. It is this realization of the inequality existing among men in the possession of the goods of the earth that explains, at least in part, the political unrest that is sweeping the earth. This revolution among men is well-known and viewed sympathetically by the Church. One conversant with the documents of Vatican II and with the statements of Pope Paul cannot help but be aware of the Church's concern for peace and for a much more equitable distribution of the world's wealth and of the world's food supply. It is part of the priesthood of the faithful to be aware of the plight of at least half of the human race and to actively promote those agencies which are struggling to achieve a lasting equity among men.

The American Christian should be scandalized, if not made sick, by the realization of the amount of money and concern lavished on pet animals in this country while men in this country and throughout the world are forced to live lives far beneath human dignity. A recent news story tells of stores which specialize in such items as mink coats for dogs, of cemeteries (with all the services normally supplied for funerals for human beings) for animals, of a company that sells health and life insurance for pets. Whatever value such things have in themselves, they are out of place in a world where almost half the human race is faced with starvation. The same newspaper article mentioned that we spend, as a nation, almost a half billion dollars a year on food for dogs. This, while millions of people in India are starving!

Christians must realize that they are their brothers' keepers. The story of the Good Samaritan is not pious fiction. The judgment-scene in the twenty-fifth chapter of St. Matthew's Gospel is not fancy. Our judgment as Christians rests on our service to others. Our priesthood is fulfilled in actively promoting peace on earth, in actively providing for our brothers those things they need in order to live lives of human dignity, and in helping them, by education and expressions of true concern, to learn to take care of themselves and to provide for their own needs.

Although the Church clearly sees the political revolution of our times, it is not immediately evident that she is as fully aware of the ramifications of other revolutions that are sweeping through human culture and affecting human evolutionary progress. If it is our duty as Christian priests to follow the lead of those whom God has appointed to be our shepherds in matters concerning social justice and equity, it is also our duty to inform these same shepherds of matters of equally vital concern to the people of God and to the whole of mankind. It is likewise our duty to press for new forms of priestly expression that will enable the Church to cope with the problems that are arising and also to press for new forms that will allow the Church to accept and use the opportunities that these cultural revolutions will present for the strengthening and growth of the kingdom of God.

There are, at present, technological, cybernetic, psychological, genetic, and moral revolutions ripping apart the fabric of human society as we know it. There are also, undoubtedly, upheavals now taking shape that are still too new to be clearly deciphered. Man's present mobility has already begun to change family life as we have known it and will, without doubt, change it more rapidly in the future. Outer space, toward which we are taking our first steps, will undoubtedly present new hazards and new opportunities to man. What lies before us in space still remains a mystery, but does that mean that the Church can afford not to concern herself with it? The genetic revolution has begun and in a few years will present the Church with problems, both of a dogmatic and a moral nature, of maximal importance and will probably also grant to the Church undreamed-of opportunities for the growth of man and of the kingdom. The same can be said of the development of the computer and of the growing science of cybernetics.

We can, it seems, hardly even imagine the changes that the human race will witness and by which the race will be transformed in the next half-century. It is absolutely necessary that the Church take these into her awareness and learn from them and impregnate them with the spirit of christic devotion to the welfare of man. Vatican II tells us that it is our duty, the duty of the whole people of God, to understand our times.

To promote such an exchange [a living exchange between the Church and the diverse cultures of people], the Church requires special help, particularly in our day, when things are changing very rapidly and the ways of thinking are exceedingly various. She must rely on those who live in the world, are versed in different institutions and specialties, and grasp their innermost significance in the eyes of both believers and unbelievers. With the help of the Holy Spirit, it is the task of the entire People of God, especially pastors and theologians, to hear, distinguish, and interpret the many voices of our age, and to judge them in the light of the divine Word. In this way, revealed truth can always be more deeply penetrated, better understood, and set forth to greater advantage (Pastoral Constitution on the Church in the Modern World, Part I, Chapter IV, Number 44).

In the following out of the Council's decree can we think of the fantastic discoveries of the past half-century as stirrings of the Spirit in the world? All these discoveries can open vast areas of opportunity for the growth of mankind and for the development of the kingdom of God. Could we perhaps consider them and the great material progress of man as a collective ecstatic speaking prompted by the Spirit? Can it be that God is opening to us, through this phenomenal series of discoveries, an avenue to a deeper understanding of the Father's plan?

But Paul tells us that ecstatic utterances must be tested and deciphered, otherwise such ecstatic speech is useless. But this speech must be interpreted and explained to the Church by those who are trained to do so and those who, dwelling in the inner life of the Triune God, are bearers of the Holy Spirit. The Church must come to understand these stirrings of all mankind. But unless some major changes are made, she will once again miss a great opportunity. If she is unwilling to live out the decrees of Vatican II, she shall have been, as she has been more than once in the past, not completely responsive to the Spirit.

The Church is not, and must never appear to be, a clerical club. While it is true that it is the pastors of the flock who must be the ultimate judges of the "signs of our times," where are they going to get the information necessary to make these judgments? It is, if we can rely on history, very unlikely that the Spirit is going to give them complete answers to questions that they do not ask. Is it sufficient for the bishops to rely only on the theologians? This has not been completely satisfactory in the past, although the situation seems better now than it has in centuries. But, in honesty, can we expect men trained solely in scripture and theology to really understand the ramifications of scientific discoveries or social changes or psychological findings? As the above citation from Vatican II says, it is the task of the entire people of God to interpret and distinguish the many voices of our age.

In fact, there is an abundant wealth of apostolic capability lying unused, and seemingly unwanted, in the Church. There are members of the Church who are highly competent in every area of human endeavor. There are Christians who have every qualification for an intensely apostolic influence both among nonbelievers and within the Church; they have everything needed to make a great contribution to the Church, everything except a ready access to and gracious audience from a segment of the theologians and the pastors of the Church. Clerics must realize that considering the faithful as children who are to be seen but not heard is a luxury that the Church can no longer afford, if she ever could afford it.

The question is, indeed, whether the Church is to take the state of the Christian priesthood seriously, or not. If she is, then she must make a real effort to utilize the training, talent, and apostolic potential of every priest, of every member of the people of God. She must search for new forms for official participation of every member of the Church in the full expression of the Christian priesthood. What might this possibly mean on the practical level?

The training, talents, and apostolic potentiality of the Christian priesthood cannot be fully exploited vis-à-vis cultural and technological problems on the parochial level or probably even on the diocesan level. The parish, set up as it is on geography, seems too disparate an entity for promoting full participation in cultural and scientific projects. The background of the parishioners is too different and their interests are too diverse to accomplish much. Then, too, the educational background of most pastors has been such that they cannot be competent, as are many of their parishioners, in matters of science, law, medicine, art, and other such professions and activities. Nor do parish duties, in general, allow them much time to pursue such an apostolate.

What is needed, perhaps, are organizations set up on the national level to promote the various professional and artistic expressions of the Christian priesthood. These need not, and should not, be considered as groupings supplanting the parish or diocese. They should be supraparochial or supradiocesan, not antiparish or antidiocesan, entities. They should consist of people with a more or less common profession and interest, under the guidance of ordained priests, or even bishops, who are trained in and deeply interested in these activities.

For example, one could envision a national organization of scientists, directed by scientists, deeply committed to the Church and to the values promoted by science. This organization would be dedicated to the spread of Christian ideals in the world of science and to informing the successors of the apostles of the problems that will soon be facing the Church and also of the tremendous opportunities which science is presenting to man and to the Church. The members of such an organization would be in a position to promote the Church's deeply committed search, along with scientists of all faiths or of no faith, into the mystery of creation. They could greatly aid in the Church's quest for at least partial answers to those perennial questions to which she must never fail to address herself.

The Church, as a pilgrim, has a great need of all the information she can get, and in our civilization much of this information is scientific in nature. Christians, organized along professional lines, could make the Church aware of the growth of knowledge and allow her time to integrate this knowledge into the revealed truth she possesses. Saint Paul mentions that it has not yet been revealed what we shall be. This could be applied to man's life on earth, merely a glimpse of which we are beginning to see now. The Church, along with mankind, will have an increasingly difficult task in coordinating the results of man's progress. A dedicated group of Christian priests, exercising their priesthood along the lines of their professional competence, can remake the face of the Church as she makes her pilgrim's way through this time of critical change.

What has been said of scientists, dedicated as scientists to the growth of the Church, can also be said of doctors, lawyers, artists, musicians, and really any group of Christians united by a common profession and competence. It must be emphasized that this is truly an expression of their baptismal priesthood. The parish does not seem to afford an entirely adequate base for this more professional or occupational aspect of the Christian priesthood. It can and should be organized along extraparochial and extradiocesan lines.

Another possible expression of this concern could be an entirely new pontifical commission for cultural advance. It would be of value to have a group of highly competent advisors to the Holy See. This group made up of men and women, clerical and nonclerical, could perform a service of great value to the Church. Were a group such as this set up, it could devote full time to probing the advances of culture and to helping all men of good will. If the members of such a group were highly trained and quite competent in their separate disciplines and if they were in close contact with the people working at all levels within these disciplines, then they could be of great assistance in informing the synod of bishops and the pope of all the ferments in and directions taken by modern culture.

The separate cultures of the world are polarizing about modern scientific and technological advances. We can, undoubtedly, look to a greater homogenization of culture in the next few decades. We can probably expect one basic cultural level with a large number of subcultures structured about it. If this should happen, we must realize that this culture will be a predominantly science-oriented culture. In this situation it would be of critical importance for the pastors of the Church to have a deep appreciation of and sympathy with whatever is of any value in these cultures. The leaders of God's people must begin to live with the problems and opportunities of today and be continually apprised of the problems and opportunities of the near future.

The Church can no longer afford to live in the past and to give quick answers to problems she does not fully understand. She cannot afford any longer to give the world answers to its problems by casting them into the categories of the thirteenth century, or of the Council of Trent, or even of Vatican I. She must learn, at her highest echelons, the new vocabulary, and she must learn to teach modern man in a way and in a language that he understands. It is an obvious truism that teaching not understood is no teaching at all.

The time has come for the Church to realize that new forms and structures are absolutely indispensable if she is to carry out her priestly mission of strengthening the kingdom and bringing it to its fullest measure of growth. She cannot stand on the beach and order the tide to wait. Human culture and human progress will not stop growing to allow her to slowly catch up. She must realize that every day she waits and does nothing to bring about a fuller expression of the Christian priesthood is a day irrevocably lost to her. We cannot afford many such days. Unless we act now, and act vigorously, we can never expect to do anymore than react to modern culture. We shall never be able to help form it and direct it.

We have suggested two possible forms that would be suited to a fuller expression of the Christian priesthood. Used in interrelation to each other these two forms would be of extreme importance in a mission of cultural penetration. The Church would then be in a position to actively join with all men of good will in the work of the conquest of nature. Were she totally involved in such work, as the servant of mankind, she would be in a better position to more effectively bring to man's will the harmony that will be essential to his proper use of his growing dominion over nature. In this way, caught up in the vision of man's control over the created universe, she could impart to man the creative vision of God as the end and goal of this control.

Then, at some point in time, when the evolving control of man over all of creation reaches its climax and includes control of man over himself for the true good of all men, a control that can be built only on the foundation of Christ's love, we shall be ready to finish our mission of completing Christ's role as ruler of all creation. That, apparently, would be the beginning. Time would merge into eternity, and Christ would return to dwell with us.

THE EUCHARISTIC EXPRESSION OF
THE PRIESTHOOD

In focusing our attention on new forms of priestly expression we must not let ourselves overlook the priestly act par excellence of the Christian priesthood, an act that has been and must continue to be the center of all priestly expression. We, of course, are speaking of the eucharistic sacrifice. This sacrament-sacrifice is the beginning and end of our priesthood, the source and climax of all our priestly life. It is here, in the union of Head and members, that the Church draws strength for her priestly mission and, at the same time, gives back to God the partial conquest of creation that has been achieved. In the Mass, the members of the Body, joined with one who shares the Headship of Christ, present to the Father, with the Son and in the Spirit, the fruit of their labor. United to the eucharistic Christ they gain strength from him and unite with his redemptive work their own work for the growth of his kingdom. All the people of God, joined in sacrifice and in the sacramental banquet, praise the Father in offering to him a greater christic domination over creation, a domination achieved in Christ by their priestly activity.

We have more clearly taught in recent years the communal features of the eucharistic mystery. We have put a greater emphasis on the fact that participation in the sacrifice and in the eucharistic banquet is more than a growth in personal union with Christ. It is a sacramentally effective bond of union of the Christian with Christ and with every member of Christ's Body. The Eucharist is, without doubt, expressive and productive of the union of the whole Body, the Head with the members and the members among themselves. In the eucharistic union the whole Church is drawn together and strengthened.

Up until the present this sacrament-sacrifice has been the major priestly exercise of the Christian. So it must remain, but hopefully it will become more apparent as time goes by that the Church has not yet used this priestly activity to its fullest extent. It has served greatly in leading Christians to a deeper union with Christ. It has proved to be a strong and fruitful element in the unification of the Church. Still, it seems as if it has not been used to consciously promote the growth of the kingdom on the cosmic level. It has been a source, and one used to great effect, of the growth of the kingdom of God in the hearts of individual Christians, which growth is an absolute essential in the achievement of Christ's mission.

Yet, this is not the sole element of that mission nor does it sum up in itself all that must yet be done by us before Christ returns to dwell with us. We have a culture to permeate with the ideals of Christ, a culture that will in time flow into even more complex cultures. It might perhaps be better to say that we have an evolving culture to convert to Christ and an evolving universe to subject to Christ. If indeed, then, the Mass is the culminating expression of our priesthood, it must be brought to bear more fully and more effectively on the cultural components of our society and on the universe as a whole. It must be the source of our power in the work of taming nature and of insuring the christic harmony of all of mankind. It must be the vehicle for our giving to the Father, for his glory and praise, that part of our mission which we have already accomplished. It must be the beginning and the end of our priestly efforts to complete Christ's messianic priesthood.

It is at least an open question whether this can be done in the parish as we know it. In the parish celebration of the eucharistic mystery each Christian can offer his individual life and work, and the whole community, as a group, can offer its growth in union with Christ. All this is proper and good. But would we not be more effective if we could at least on occasions be unified, perhaps, along professional lines? What would this mean? Among other things it would involve the coming together in the eucharistic Christ of a group who are similarly dedicated to the conquest of nature in a certain discipline.

In union with each other, a union built on Christ's presence in the Eucharist, these men can draw for their profession and for their own professional lives from the power of Christ. In faith they can come to realize that their mutual union with Christ will bring the blessing of God on their corporate effort to affect man's progress and to build a world where each man has the opportunity to live a life worthy of his true dignity. In faith they can become consciously aware of the power of God being brought to bear on the successful accomplishment of their professional goal and ideal. They will become more deeply convinced of God's working in and through their daily effort for greater domination of and progress in the world. They, then, through their common sharing in the eucharistic Christ, will strengthen the dynamic Christ who still grows toward maturity.

It is in the Eucharist where, by the sacramental dedication of a common work for the progress of mankind and for the growth of the kingdom of God, the Christian professional will do his part in union with others in fulfilling the words of St. Paul.

And to some, his gift was that they should be apostles; to some, prophets; to some, evangelists; to some, pastors and teachers; so that the saints together make a unity in the work of service, building up the body of Christ. In this way we are all to come to unity in our faith and in our knowledge of the Son of God, until we become the perfect Man, fully mature with the fulness of Christ himself. (Eph. 4:11-13).

In the eucharistic Christ, men dedicated to Christ through their work can offer to the Father the results of their common effort to promote man's progress. The Spirit apportions his gifts to a man's ability, inclinations, and training. Grouped in common about the Eucharist as the center of their total lives—of their personal and professional lives— Christians can offer to the Father the fruit of their common effort. They can, in union with Christ and in union with each other, offer the sacrifice of their professional activity in a dynamic and effective manner. What is true of an individual living in the Spirit should be true of a group which is consciously working toward the Father in the Spirit. They can expect, then, that the Spirit will plead with the Father for the success of their activity in behalf of the growing dominion of Christ over all things.

It is in the eucharistic offering that we may see one of the prime reasons for the ordained being engaged with the faithful in every legitimate human occupation. For the ordained priest who is involved, for instance, in scientific research can join with other Christian priests in offering to God their common work for the kingdom of God. Then, in the union of Head and members a segment of the Church offers, in the name of the whole Church, its area of concern for creation to the Father. In this union of ordained and nonordained priests, engaged in a common mission toward man and creation, the whole Church offers to the Father its concern for man's progress and for all of creation, and in the offering it sacramentally achieves a further step in the submission of all things to the Father.

In faith we know that we effect in the Mass the continuing sacrificial offering of Christ to the Father, an offering that is most pleasing to the Father. This sacrifice when offered to the Father on Calvary effected the redemption of all of creation. Now, when offered by the ordained priest, it brings the continuing total redemptive power of Christ to bear on the mission of the Church. Through the union of the ordained and nonordained it would seem that the redeeming power of Christ would more fully be brought to bear on the activity of those joined together by their common concern for the penetration of a particular area of the culture.

In brief, we should look to an understanding of the ordained priesthood in the context of the baptismal priesthood rather than seeking an understanding of the baptismal priesthood in terms of the priesthood of orders. This should open up the theological vision of the baptismal priesthood. It hopefully would broaden the scope of this priestly state so that its mission would become coextensive with the mission of the Church. It makes little sense to restrict the priestly mission of the people of God to a purely liturgical participation in the worship of God.

If the people of God have the priestly obligation of sanctifying, teaching, and ruling themselves, the Church, and all creation, they truly have the right to the full expression of that priesthood. They have the right to be truly and effectively served in that mission by those who have been chosen by God to aid them. They have the right to have that help present to them in every area of their priestly lives in the way that they need it. If they do not have a right to the full aid of the ordained priesthood in the totality of their lives, in their professional as well as in their personal endeavors, then they can have no priestly obligation to promote the growth of the kingdom of God in the part of creation that they touch. If they have no priestly obligations, then it is non-sense to talk about the priestly people of God.

The whole theology of the Christian priesthood has yet to be worked out. This book merely represents a tentative ap-proach to the question. If there is any value in this treat-ment, then we must look to the baptismal priesthood for deeper insights into the meaning of the priesthood in gen-eral. The baptismal priesthood has meaning only in the priestly mission of Christ, a mission as broad as the universe itself. The day has long passed when we can afford the dubi-ous luxury of considering the faithful as passive spectators in the priestly activity of the Church, as some sort of second class Christians, or as watered-down clerics.

The layman is the bulwark of the Church, to be respected as such and to be listened to as such. Granted that he does not have official authority in governing the people of God, still it is for his benefit and for the benefit of the people of God that this authority is given to anyone. It is certainly not given for the enhancement of the position and power of the bishops and other members of the hierarchy. It is given to guide and to serve, not to promote a given structure or a given bureaucracy. It is not given to "lay burdens on men and then not to lift a finger to help men carry them." There can be no doubt from scripture that authority means service in the Church. It is heresy to presume that the hierarchy alone is led by the Spirit. The faithful are fully priests by virtue of their baptism and are to be respected as such and, of course, must conduct themselves as such.

Priests are mediators between God and man and between God and all of creation. Their task, their mission, is to bring God to all of reality and all of reality to God. Every Christian shares this task, a task for the accomplishment of which all creation groans in anguish. It is our Christian mission that we accomplish the "new state of things" that Paul speaks of. Our priesthood is as wide as the cosmos and as narrow as ourselves. It encompasses everything. It looks to everything. It must accomplish everything so that Christ, whose priests we all are, "should be first in everyway."